THE INSPIRED LEADER: REVIEWS

'An excellent and uplifting book that provides genuine insight into how leaders of all types can understand what truly motivates them and how they can use this to inspire others. Given the intense personal pressures facing so many people in business today, I recommend it as a highly relevant and compelling read whatever your level of experience.'

CAROLYN FAIRBAIRN, *Director-General, Confederation of British Industry*

'This is a wonderful book – I am falling in love with it. I read it and I feel better about humanity, about being a member of this funny old thing called the "human race." Why 'race'? The people Andy Bird writes about become more human by stopping still, by getting to know themselves better. They give up on racing and become who they are. It is a celebration of humanity, and if that isn't inspirational I don't know what is.'

ALISON HARDINGHAM, *Professor, Henley Business School*

'Andy Bird's uncommon combination of intellect, experience and values has created a powerful, timely and unique work. Insightful and actionable frameworks, illuminated by inspiring leadership stories, invite us to reflect deeply on how we can inspire ourselves to become more effective leaders – not just of our own organizations, but in the world at large.'

MATT SHATTOCK, *CEO & Chairman, Beam Suntory Inc.*

'Unlike other books I've read in the genre, this one offers a realistic and relatable way to improving leadership qualities. The ideas and evidence provided show how, by being proactive in seeking the right sources of motivation, it is possible to become inspired to realise your potential. As a young professional, this book has also made me question my own perception of "success" – something invaluable when setting my long-term personal and career-related goals at this stage in my life.'

YIANNIS GEORGIOU, *Associate, PwC*

'Inspiration is at the heart of strong leadership, but where does it come from? This book unlocks our thinking about how we can find the drive in ourselves consistently to inspire others. I wish I had read it 40 years ago.'

GENERAL SIR PETER WALL, *former Chief of the General Staff, British Army*

'Inspiring and bold. Andy Bird demonstrates how we can be at our best more of the time and motivate others to do the same. Leadership at its best.'

GEMMA GREAVES, *Chief Executive, The Marketing Society*

'When leaders know their purpose, when they are inspired, the human spark in them is ignited. This leads to a greater sense of wellbeing for them and their teams, better business performance and ultimately a better world. I am happy to see that this book focuses on helping leaders do just that. I highly recommend this essential, purposeful work.'

LEENA NAIR, *Chief HR Officer, Unilever*

'Combining the ancient art of story-telling with cutting edge insights from behavioural science, this book provides a powerful roadmap for connecting more with what inspires you. The practical reflective exercises at the end of each chapter give the book a real feel that you are sitting in on a masterclass. Inspirational reading.'

PAUL HEARDMAN, *Leadership Coach & Coaching Supervisor, UK Civil Service*

'To inspire others you first need to BE inspired ... and this book does exactly that. Packed with inspiration, wisdom, tools and insight, it's like having your own personal leadership guru on hand at all times. Read from cover to cover, digest it all and then become the leader you want to be. At last, a leadership handbook for everyone.'

SHERILYN SHACKELL, *Founder & CEO,*
The Marketing Academy

THE INSPIRED LEADER

THE INSPIRED LEADER

*How leaders can discover,
experience and maintain
their inspiration*

ANDY BIRD

Bloomsbury Business
An imprint of Bloomsbury Publishing Plc

B L O O M S B U R Y
LONDON • OXFORD • NEW YORK • NEW DELHI • SYDNEY

Bloomsbury Business

An imprint of Bloomsbury Publishing Plc

50 Bedford Square	1385 Broadway
London	New York
WC1B 3DP	NY 10018
UK	USA

www.bloomsbury.com

**BLOOMSBURY and the Diana logo are trademarks
of Bloomsbury Publishing Plc**

First published 2018

© Andy Bird, 2018

British Library Cataloguing-in-Publication Data

A catalogue record for this book is available from the British Library.

ISBN: PB: 978-1-4729-4792-5
ePDF: 978-1-4729-4793-2
ePub: 978-1-4729-4791-8

Library of Congress Cataloging-in-Publication Data

Library of Congress Cataloging-in-Publication Data
Names: Bird, Andy, author.
Title: The inspired leader: how leaders can discover, experience and
maintain their inspiration / by Andy Bird.
Description: London; New York, NY: Bloomsbury Business, 2017. | Includes
bibliographical references and index.
Identifiers: LCCN 2017026989 (print) | LCCN 2017038894 (ebook) | ISBN 9781472947932
(ePDF) | ISBN 9781472947918 (ePub) | ISBN 9781472947949
(eXML) | ISBN 9781472947925 (pbk.)
Subjects: LCSH: Leadership. | Inspiration.
Classification: LCC HD57.7 (ebook) | LCC HD57.7 .B53465 2017 (print) | DDC 658.4/092–dc23
LC record available at https://lccn.loc.gov/2017026989

Cover design by Kerry Squires
Cover image © Getty Images

Typeset by Deanta Global Publishing Services, Chennai, India
Printed and bound in Great Britain

To find out more about our authors and books visit www.bloomsbury.com. Here you will
find extracts, author interviews, details of forthcoming events and the option
to sign up for our newsletters.

Brand Learning Group Ltd, part of Accenture, owns all rights relating to the trademark 'Brand
Learning', which is reproduced with its kind permission.

CONTENTS

YOUR FIRST AND FOREMOST JOB AS A LEADER
IS TO TAKE CHARGE OF YOUR OWN ENERGY
AND THEN HELP TO ORCHESTRATE
THE ENERGY OF THOSE AROUND YOU.

PETER DRUCKER

Introduction

Can you remember a time when you felt inspired? Perhaps you were influenced by a person you met, admiring them for their courage, compassion or integrity. For some of us it may have been some form of religious experience or a magnificent encounter with the natural world. Or was it a time when you felt a sense of pride in having achieved something particularly challenging or meaningful?

The feelings that come with these moments can be wonderfully invigorating. A lifting of the spirit and a surge in our energy and vitality. An exciting sense of possibility and a renewed belief in ourselves and everything that life has to offer.

In fact, given how much we value and enjoy inspiration, it is surprising how little we actually know about it. Are all forms of inspiration the same? Is it something we have to wait for in the hope it might arrive now and again? How can we each take steps to experience inspiration more intensely and frequently in our lives?

These are some of the important questions this book will address. And there is no one for whom they are more significant than people who take on the responsibility of being a leader.

We are living in a tumultuous world – economic volatility, digital disruption, terrorism, climate change, Trump, Brexit. The extraordinary pace and scale of change we are experiencing is creating a host of thrilling opportunities, but also some unnerving threats for people and organizations everywhere. These conditions are creating an urgent need for talented individuals to step up and influence what is going on around them in beneficial ways. Driving change that makes a positive difference in the world is what being a leader is all about.

Doing so in reality, though, is far from easy. The same turbulent conditions also make the personal challenges facing people in leadership roles greater than ever before. Many recent studies and examples point to the high levels of stress and burnout being experienced by people in senior positions. The unrelenting demand for outstanding results, combined with excessive workloads and emotional pressures, is clearly taking its toll.

These personal trials are heightened by the fact that, in today's complex organizations, the command-and-control approach many leaders have traditionally used to make things happen is breaking down. The social media-fuelled desire among both customers and employees for greater transparency and involvement in corporate affairs also means that it has become increasingly necessary to lead without relying on hierarchical authority. Leaders must now focus more on building influence with others by inspiring and engaging them, rather than by simply telling them what to do.

But it would be a mistake to start by going down the well-trodden route of exploring how leaders can get better at inspiring *others*. I believe the time has come to pay greater attention to helping leaders discover first the inspiration and energy they need *for themselves*.

If individuals are to take on all the responsibility and pressure that leadership can entail, they need to be fuelled upfront by a deep passion to drive change in the world around them. If they are to inspire belief and commitment in the hearts and minds of others, they must first find these qualities in their own hearts and minds.

Being an inspired leader

The purpose of this book is to help you explore what inspires *you* as a leader. How can you enjoy the uplifting sensation of inspiration more regularly in your life? How can you sustain your energy in the face of the inevitable adversity that arises? And how can you be moved to make a bigger difference through the leadership role you play?

Inspired leaders feel exhilarated by getting deeply involved in work they are passionate about. They embrace exciting challenges that enable them to apply and grow their distinctive personal talents. They derive a greater sense of meaning in their lives by finding ways to uphold the values they care about and believe in.

The ultimate result is that being an inspired leader provides each of us with opportunities to make the most of ourselves as human beings, and thereby maximize our positive impact on the people and the world around us.

This stirring opportunity is not just relevant for people in senior management roles. You may be leading a small team early in your career, or running a local club or project far removed from your life at work. The key point is that inspired leaders are needed *throughout* our companies, institutions and communities if we are all to thrive in the face of the dramatic changes going on around us.

My own leadership story

I have a clear memory, from just over 30 years ago, of sitting in a rather nondescript university meeting room and being gripped suddenly by an acute sense of excitement and possibility. At the time, I had no idea what I wanted to do as a career and the end of my student life was approaching fast.

A team from Proctor & Gamble had come along to run a session explaining what marketing was all about, in the hope of attracting a group of potential graduate recruits. The exercise they took us through that evening ignited an interest in me that changed the direction of my life. There was something in the way they expressed the essence of marketing that really caught my imagination. I was captivated by the thought of trying to discover insight into what motivates people, and then responding with creative ideas for brands, new products and communication.

A few months later, I accepted an offer to join Unilever's marketing training scheme (which I'm sure wasn't quite what P&G had intended!). I spent the next fifteen years working for them in the UK, Singapore and India and loved many aspects of the experience. However, it wasn't always easy and I battled with a fair bit of stress at times too. I had my share of inspiring bosses, but also of demotivating ones, and I learned first-hand the impact this can have on one's personal spirit.

Towards the end of this period, I decided to take an unconventional career step and pursued what seemed an extremely interesting opportunity to help review Unilever's approach to building its global marketing capabilities. I went on to set up and lead their Marketing Academy and soon realized that the focus for my passion had shifted. Rather than wanting to be a marketing practitioner myself, I was finding it even more rewarding to be seeking out the secrets behind great marketing and bringing these to life for other people within the organization.

Early in 2000, the inspiration for my next career step arrived in the unexpected form of a gin and tonic and a conversation on a flight to New York. It is amazing what effect combining a bit of alcohol and altitude can have on the entrepreneurial spirit! An idea began to crystallize of leaving Unilever to set up a new business focused on helping a broader range of companies strengthen their marketing capabilities. By the end of that year Mhairi McEwan and I, together with Mark Simmonds, a founding colleague in the initial few months, had set out on the first steps of a journey via which Brand Learning grew into a thriving global consultancy firm.

In partnership with our outstanding leadership team, our vision was to create a company that was commercially successful, but that also had an inclusive and collaborative culture enabling people to truly be themselves. An exciting recent development has been Brand Learning's acquisition by Accenture, a move that is now opening up many new opportunities for its clients, its people and its business.

As my own experience has grown, I have found my focus has evolved further. In recent years, my passion to explore ideas and support people's learning has progressed from the technical territory of marketing to the more personal area of leadership.

The path to this book

I have now had the privilege of providing leadership consultancy and coaching support to hundreds of leaders in a diverse range of organizations. This work has left me fascinated by the unquenchable thirst people seem to have for inspiration. I have also seen the fantastic impact that uplifting experiences, stories and role models can sometimes have on their energy levels.

As a result, some time ago I began channelling this interest into a research project at Henley Business School to look at how people discover and maintain the inspiration they need to lead large businesses. More recently I have extended this work by conducting further research with a wide range of leaders in other walks of life, including education, the arts, religion, government, sport, the police and the armed forces.

I have been struck by how little academic research has been done to date to understand what it is that motivates leaders. The work that has been undertaken has focused mainly on serving the interests of the corporate and military organizations people work for, seeking to find correlations between individual motivation profiles and future leadership performance.

My objective in writing this book is to redirect this effort and provide more personal support for leaders themselves. In many ways, the inspiration I experienced myself all those years ago as a student is still playing out. My sincere hope is that the ideas I share in the coming pages will help you discover insight into *your* motivation, and perhaps even influence, in some small way, the direction your own life is taking.

Headlines on what to expect

Inspiration has an elusive quality. Just like happiness, the risk is that the more we concentrate on trying to achieve it, the further from reach it can become. However, emerging from my research into the real-life experiences of leaders is one overriding and intriguing insight:

*The secret to discovering leadership inspiration lies in better appreciating our relationship with **time** and the role it plays in our lives as human beings.*

Like it or not, our time on earth is limited. Deep within each of us is a desire to make the most of it and to give our lives as much meaning as possible.

As time ticks by, our experience of the past and all that has happened builds up behind us. The future, on the other hand, continues to stretch ahead, with all its limitless possibilities. Our great challenge as individuals is to draw the most out of what we have learned and who we have become, up to the present moment, in order that we can make the most of all the time we have remaining. And that in turn involves making the most of every present moment, the only point at which we ever actually experience time in reality.

The exciting news is that inspiration does not have to happen by accident. In **Part 1** of the book, we will learn how to **discover** inspiration more intensely and more frequently as our lives unfold.

I will explain the alchemy of inspiration, a magical interaction that takes place over time between the three critical elements necessary for inspiration to occur. The first is our *internal motivations*, the psychological needs that influence what we find most appealing and rewarding as individuals. Our next focus will be on the *mindsets* we bring to *engage* with the world and interpret our experience within it. Finally we will look at the *external triggers* in our environment – the events, people and circumstances that can stimulate our feelings of inspiration.

My research has also identified four different ways in which leaders can **experience** inspiration in practice, each determined by our relative place in time. I will explain these states in **Part 2**, describing the distinctive feelings and benefits involved.

The first is a sense of *purpose*, which comes from a desire to make a positive difference in the world *in the future*. The second is a sense of *enjoyment*, which comes from the passion we can feel for the work being done *in the present*. Third is a sense of *achievement,* which comes after seeing positive results from our efforts *in the past.* And finally, *beyond* this time continuum, we can be enlightened by a sense of *illumination* that has the power to change our perspective on the kind of person we can be and the leadership role we can play.

Becoming inspired is one thing, but staying inspired over time is perhaps even more challenging. In **Part 3**, our focus will move to the techniques leaders can use to **maintain** their inspiration, not just from moment to moment, but over the course of a lifetime. We will conclude by reflecting on the lessons to be drawn from our own inspiration as individuals, and the implications for the way we can better inspire the people we are seeking to lead.

To help you navigate your way through the book, the roadmap in Figure 1 explains the structure of these three parts and the flow between the twelve chapters.

DISCOVER	
1	The Alchemy of Inspiration
2	Internal Motivations
3	Engaging Mindsets
4	External Triggers

EXPERIENCE	
5	The Inspiration Timeline
6	Future Purpose
7	Present Enjoyment
8	Past Achievement
9	Illumination Beyond Time

MAINTAIN	
10	Sources of Resilience
11	Inspiration over a Lifetime
12	Inspiring Others

FIGURE 1 *Chapter Roadmap.*

In each chapter, I provide a range of leadership stories and concepts to stimulate your thinking. Most importantly, though, the role of the book is intended to help you consider your own experiences and inspiration. At the end of every chapter, a set of questions has been provided to guide your reflection.

Taking some time to think things through for yourself in this way will hopefully provide a valuable opportunity for you to develop a deeper level of self-awareness and understanding.

The questions are also designed to help you create some very practical plans to increase your chances of feeling more inspired, more of the time.

I am conscious that some readers may want to find out more for themselves about the ideas referred to. To keep the book accessible and easy to read, the extensive academic references that lie behind it have not been highlighted throughout the text. Instead, to help guide your own research, I have listed the sources for each chapter in the 'References' section at the back and made suggestions about books and articles that you might find particularly useful. Further resources, blog posts and leadership interviews are also available via my website www.andybird.com

As will soon become clear, the path to inspiration is primarily an internal one. I hope that the combination of my written materials and the opportunity for your own guided discovery will prove genuinely inspiring for you personally.

Thank You

I am indebted to a large number of leaders who have helped contribute towards my research for this book. I would like to acknowledge, in particular, the generosity of the following people in sharing their experiences in a spirit of such honesty and humility.

I regret that I have not been able to include quotes and stories from every individual listed, but all have played a significant role in helping to shape the conclusions I have reached. My selection here has been driven primarily by a desire to maintain an appropriate balance between the various roles, nationalities and ages of the leaders featured. More detailed interviews with some of the contributors can be found at www.andybird.com

Rev. Alistair Tressider, Prior to St. Luke's Church, Hampstead

Anne-Lise Johnsen, Youth Product Manager, Arsenal F.C.

Claire Chiang, Co-Founder, Banyan Tree Hotels & Resorts

David Bunch, Vice President – Marketing, Shell

Declan Donnellan, Theatre Director and Co-Founder, Cheek By Jowl

Dominic Murphy, Member & Head of UK & Ireland, KKR

Doug Howlet, former Captain, Munster R.F.C and All Black rugby player

Dr. Edward L. Deci, Professor of Psychology, University of Rochester

Eric Tornoe, Global Team Leader, Pfizer

Gary Hilton, former Superintendent, Merseyside Police; Founder, Coaching 4 Better Performance

Ian Cranna, Vice President, EMEA, Starbucks

Rev. Inderjit Bhogal OBE, President, City of Sanctuary & Methodist Peace Fellowship

James Brett, Founder, Plant for Peace

Jan Gooding, Global Inclusion Director, Aviva and Chair, Stonewall

Jon Harding, Managing Director – Global Head of Senior Leadership Group Talent & Development, Barclays

Josh Boutwood, Corporate Executive Chef, Bistro Group

Juergen Maier, Chief Executive Officer, Siemens UK

Julia Finch, City Editor, The Guardian

Juliette Howell, Joint-CEO, House Productions

Kerris Bright, Chief Marketing Officer, Virgin Media

Dr. Kiat W. Tan, Chief Executive Officer, Gardens by the Bay, Singapore

Lawrence Dallaglio, former Captain, Wasps and England rugby teams

Lisa Anson, President, AstraZeneca UK

Martin George, Customer Director, Waitrose

Matt Dean, Founder, byrne·dean

Molly Watt, Founder, Molly Watt Trust

Murray Harper, Global Head of Change Management, HSBC

Niall FitzGerald KBE, Chairman, Leverhulme Trust, Munster R.F.C and Brand Learning; former Chairman, Unilever and Reuters

Nihal Kaviratne CBE, Chairman – India, AkzoNobel

Dr. Patricia Riddell, Professor of Applied Neuroscience, School of Psychology and CLS, University of Reading

Patrick Spence, President, Sonos

Paul O'Connell, former Captain, Munster R.F.C., Ireland and British Lions & Irish

Phyll Opoku-Gyimah, Executive Director and Co-Founder, Black Pride

Rebecca Hill, Director, Ernst & Young

General Sir Richard Dannatt, former Chief of the General Staff, British Army

Roger Burge, Corporate Finance Director, Arqiva

Sabrina Zurkuhlen, Head of Athletics Dept., The Calhoun School, New York City

Sarah Ellis, Head of Marketing Strategy, Sainsbury's; Founder of Amazing If and Inspire

Simon Lowden, President – Global Snacks Group, PepsiCo

Sir Richard Branson, Founder, Virgin Group

Tom Willis, Security Director, Heathrow Airport

Usain Bolt, Jamaican sprinter and Olympic champion

Dr. Vanessa Ogden, Head Teacher, Mulberry School for Girls, Tower Hamlets

Zaid Al-Qassab, Chief Brand Officer, BT

PART ONE

HOW LEADERS CAN *DISCOVER* INSPIRATION

DISCOVER		EXPERIENCE	MAINTAIN
1	The Alchemy of Inspiration		
2	Internal Motivations		
3	Engaging Mindsets		
4	External Triggers		

WE SEE THINGS NOT AS THEY ARE,
BUT AS WE ARE OURSELVES.

H. M. TOMLINSON

1

DISCOVER	
1	The Alchemy of Inspiration
2	Internal Motivations
3	Engaging Mindsets
4	External Triggers

On 26 December 1988, six months through her pregnancy, Claire Chiang was rushed to hospital and admitted to intensive care. Over the next four weeks, the doctors did all they could to save the lives of both her and her baby. In her case they were successful but, tragically, not in the case of her child. The fight was finally lost on 19 January and Claire was devastated.

'I had this tremendous feeling that I had failed as a woman. I felt such guilt. I hadn't wanted my baby enough and therefore it left me,' Claire recounts. 'It was very hard hitting for me, because no one understood. It was my third child, so everyone just said: "It's a miscarriage – these things happen." But that's not how I saw it. No words could comfort me. For me, my baby was my blood and I had failed it.'

At this point in her life, Claire had been a highly respected academic, teaching in the Sociology Department of the National University of Singapore. Following her bereavement, she entered a period of severe depression. 'I closed down and rejected the world,' she recalls. 'I literally wasn't able to speak to anyone. I started using sign language and I began healing in a world of silence.'

The following months proved to be an extremely painful period for Claire. However, as time passed, she gradually found a way of coming to terms with what had happened to her. She began to emerge with a very different perspective on her life and a remarkable change was soon underway in the profile and scope of her activities.

If we jump forward for a moment to 1994, Claire had taken on the leadership of the Association of Women for Action and Research (AWARE), an organization championing gender equality in Singapore. The following year she also became president of the Society against Family Violence. As her profile as a social activist increased, Claire was soon one of the first women to be invited to become a Nominated Member of Parliament, serving two terms between 1997 and 2001. She was also one of only two women admitted to the Council of the Singapore Chamber of Commerce and Industry in its ninety-year history. In 1999 she was named Singapore's 'Woman of the Year' for her contribution to the community.

Since then, Claire Chiang has gone on to live an incredibly varied life as a leader. Together with her husband, the renowned journalist Ho Kwon Ping, she founded the Banyan Tree resort hotel chain and has established it as a pioneering force in the sphere of corporate social responsibility. She has chaired many boards and government councils, including the National Book Development Council, Wildlife Reserves Singapore and the ACCORD Family & Community Council. Claire's current directorships include positions on the boards of the Singapore Art Museum, ISS A/S in Denmark and Dufry AG in Switzerland. Her impressive leadership impact has been acknowledged again recently with the Public Service Star in Singapore and the award of Woman Entrepreneur of the Year in Asia.

How did Claire discover the inspiration to recover from such a difficult personal crisis and become such a passionate leader across so many different causes and enterprises? And what can we learn from her experience to help us discover our own sources of leadership inspiration?

The magical process of inspiration

Before we can answer these questions properly, we first need to take a step back and reflect on what we mean by inspiration and how it actually occurs.

In literal terms, inspiration relates to the drawing in of breath required to give life to our physical bodies. In common parlance, we now use the word more frequently to describe the way ideas and experiences infuse life into our *spirit* as human beings. To be inspired means to feel fully alive, to experience a surge in our life force, to be motivated positively both to *do* and to *be* certain things in our lives.

The title of this chapter – the *alchemy* of inspiration – was chosen for a reason. Alchemy is a term that relates to a seemingly magical process of transmutation, creation or combination, a description that captures very well what happens when we personally feel inspired. Let me explain.

In my work running leadership development programmes, we often invite senior leaders to join us and share their personal stories and insights. What is noticeable is that the delegates sometimes have very different views about which people they find most inspiring. The fact is that there is nothing *inherent* about any individual that makes them inspiring as a person. It is the characteristics they possess which are *interpreted* as being inspiring, to a greater or lesser extent, in the eyes of the people they encounter.

The same is true of experiences. Reading a particular book or watching a film may have a lasting impact on us personally, but the same stimulus may often leave other people completely cold. Engaging in certain types of enjoyable activity at work might light our own fire but, for some people, having to do the same task might well be their worst nightmare.

Inspiration takes place in a unique way for each of us as individuals when three elements come together in a magical way:

- The *triggers* we encounter in the external world – the situations, events and people we experience as we progress through our lives.
- The *mindsets* we bring to interpret these experiences and relate them to our own selves.
- The *motivations* we feel internally, especially the values, interests and talents we have most passion for.

Inspiration results when our engagement with the world touches us in a special and uplifting manner. The reason different *triggers* have a different impact on each of us is that we all relate to them in different ways. Our *mindsets* play a critical role in shaping how we understand and make meaning of our experiences. The way they then resonate with us depends upon the extent to which they connect with our deepest *motivations*.

Now let us return to the story of Claire Chiang to see how the alchemy of inspiration took place for her in reality.

The connection between triggers and mindsets

Back at the start of 1989, Claire spent three months in a state of withdrawal from the world, trying to make sense of the loss of her baby and what she had done to deserve it. However, the passage of time soon began to play its part. The point came when she began to feel a need to start reconnecting with the human voice and so she applied to join the Samaritans of Singapore (SOS). Despite some concern about her preparedness for the role, she was able to persuade the counsellors interviewing her that her recent personal crisis would enable her to empathize well with the pain of other people looking for support.

'For four years I served on the hotline, hearing about other people's issues, fears and delusions,' Claire remembers. 'I began to realize the problems were so often about them being enslaved to a perception of who they were as people. We all tell ourselves stories about "I am this" or "I am that." Much of my work was about helping people find other ways of thinking about themselves.'

These experiences served as an invaluable inspirational *trigger* for Claire. As time progressed, she began to discover a new way of interpreting her own circumstances. 'I was telling myself about my own failure and my lost sense of womanhood, but then I hear from another woman about *her* miscarriage. And

I realize this is not just about me – this can be a biological defect; it happens in life. So I switched my mindset from one based on the question "Why me?" to one that asked instead "Why *not* me?"' she explains.

The shift in her *mindset* from a sense of injustice and being a victim, to one of greater acceptance, helped to transform her perspective on life. 'I realized that I am just one of a zillion people, so why should I *not* be one of the very few people who suffer this kind of experience? It was humbling and reductionist, but it was incredibly liberating. It helped me to walk away from my imprisoned self and to re-embrace the world.'

Although Claire never fully lost the sense of pain that came from losing her baby, she began to find a way of loosening the grip it had on her. 'The journey of activism I embarked upon helped give me further experiences that enabled me to substitute the painful memories with new, more positive ones,' she reflects.

'I truly believe there are opportunities all around us, but sometimes we just don't see them,' she goes on. 'The reason our mindset is so important is that we have to look for the connections and the possibilities in front of us.'

One particular moment of illumination came for Claire when she met an exceptional lady called Shirin Fozdar, a champion of women's rights and education in Asia. At the time, Claire and her husband were in the process of building their first Banyan Tree spa hotel on the island of Phuket in Thailand.

'Shirin came to me with two cushions and she said that if I bought them for our hotel, my money would help put a girl in school,' Claire recalls. 'I thought – 2 cushions, 1 girl in school; 200 cushions, 100 girls; 2000 cushions, you can save a whole village. That was the trigger that changed my whole perspective on business and the role it can play as a force for social good.'

As a consequence, Claire went on to build up the international Banyan Tree operation in a way that supports the artisanal crafts and village communities where it has a presence. The group's purpose is firmly rooted in a commitment to contribute towards the sustainable physical and human development of the environments where its hotels are situated.

The role of motivations

Just as Claire's perspectives on the world around her continued to evolve as time passed, so too did the way she viewed *herself*. 'After a while, I began to see myself differently again,' she explains. 'From: "Why me?," to: "Why *not* me?" and then simply to: "*It's me*." I have become more centred in who I am and what I believe in; I'm more accepting of myself and what I can bring.'

Claire's inspiration as a leader over time has been driven by some deep *motivations*. Her commitment to a core set of values and beliefs has been the underlying fuel for her passionate community activism and authentic leadership. 'When people ask me about why I've done all these things, it's because I believe in them – I believe in the causes,' she declares. 'I believe in justice, in the independence of women. I believe women should be educated. I believe in marriage, family and the power of community.'

'Values are the ultimate foundation, but that begs the question which values?' Claire reflects. 'I say put away all those values that can differentiate, because differentiators can become discriminators. I believe in the core human values, the ones that bring us together, rather than tear us apart – openness, compassion, inclusiveness, honesty, justice and honour. These things are about bringing goodness to the world, about not harming each other, about sharing and unity. That's what I believe in.'

As the scope of Claire's role and influence has expanded, she has also had the chance to focus on doing the things she is good at and the things she most enjoys. 'As I took on all the responsibilities, they were opportunities for me to express myself and to exhibit my talents,' she admits. The strengths she sees in herself include characteristics such as intensity, earnestness, resilience and delivering on her duties.

'I love being able to compose things through the opportunities that are given to me – composing speeches, composing motions in parliament, composing business models.' And in a way, it is through these very activities that Claire seems to have found a way to compose her own self. 'It's through embracing all that is available out there that I can be me – Claire.'

Rising to the highest level, what does Claire see as the point to her life? How would she describe her ultimate sense of purpose?

'I am an atheist, so I have no notion of my life as being beholden to the call or order of a God,' she confides. 'I live in a responsible manner as a humanist. If I were to put it in the economic terms of the Financial Times, I do my best to make the most of the capital I have been given by my mother! I *am* the capital and I live to maximize and multiply myself as best I can.'

The essence of leadership inspiration

To maximize and multiply myself as best I can. What a fascinating turn of phrase. Set aside for a moment what Claire says about her atheist beliefs – many of the leaders I have met differ from her in having a very strong religious faith. However, what unites them all is this burning desire to make the most of who they are as individuals and the positive impact they can have in the world.

This insight sheds important light on the very essence of leadership inspiration. The lift in spirits that we experience, the aspiration we associate with certain values, the motivation we feel to drive change. All these factors seem to arise when we discover *an opportunity to enhance the sense we have of our selves*

*as human beings and the potential beneficial difference we can
make beyond our selves.*

We must explore this thought in more detail. Psychologists
point out that our sense of self has a number of dimensions.
From one perspective, it is all about us as individuals – a complex
bundle of perceptions, stories and beliefs that influence what we
think and know about ourselves. However, we do not and cannot
exist in isolation. From another perspective we can only fully
understand ourselves through the way we relate to other people.
We define ourselves as much by comparing ourselves with others
as we do by knowing ourselves in our own right.

Crucially, though, we don't just *exist* as individuals or even as
social beings – we can *act* too. A third dimension to our sense
of self involves appreciating our ability to make choices, take
actions and influence our environment. This is where the fact that
we exist in the context of *time* becomes so significant. It means
we have the extraordinary opportunity to improve ourselves, to
develop our capabilities and to increase our influence beyond
ourselves as our lives progress.

The importance of time

Patricia Riddell is a professor of applied neuroscience and has
held senior academic posts in the psychology departments

of Brooklyn College and Columbia University in the United States and Reading University in the United Kingdom. 'I'm really interested in the role of time because it's something I haven't seen highlighted in quite this way before,' observes Patricia. 'What I think you're pointing to is that people feel inspired when they have an opportunity to grow and expand their sense of self, and that's only possible when you bring in the dimension of time.'

'Once you've seen you're capable of achieving something, it gives you the confidence to take on another challenge, and then another,' she continues. 'It's particularly powerful if your achievement goes beyond what you thought you were capable of, in which case there will be a drive to do it again and achieve even more.'

'Just thinking about it, I can even relate this to my own experience,' Patricia reflects. 'When I finished my PhD at Oxford – which I didn't believe I'd ever actually get! – my most important learning was that I could learn *anything*. It wasn't about the content of the PhD itself, it was the change in frame that I now knew I had the competence *to learn*. That was an incredibly important moment for me in my career as an academic.'

In summary, then, leadership inspiration seems to involve, at its heart, an uplifting sense of opportunity to make the most of all our potential qualities and capabilities in the time available to us as human beings. In doing so, we are able to channel our values and passions to make the biggest possible impact on the world around us, bringing greater significance to our lives as a result.

Seek and you shall find

Claire Chiang's story provides a rich illustration of the way our experiences, mindsets and motivations can combine over time to enable us to lead a more inspired life as a leader. Despite the fact she suffered such a distressing bereavement when she was younger, her willingness to embrace the world and to broaden her experience helped bring about a major shift in the direction of her life.

Many of the moments of illumination she experienced during her journey arrived unexpectedly. The insight she had about the potential social role of the Banyan Tree business during her meeting with Shirin Fozdar is a great example. But these moments came to her in large part because she had a mindset that was *seeking* opportunities to make a difference in the world.

Similarly, her growing sense of self-awareness and authenticity arose because she was *seeking* to learn about herself from the experiences she was going through. 'I see this as a continuing process of maturation,' Claire explains. 'We should be continually looking to feed back our experiences, to build on our foundations and to move our knowledge of ourselves on to a higher level. I see it as a journey of lifelong learning, of being and becoming.'

There is certainly a wonderful, magical dimension to the alchemy of inspiration. It is not a feeling we can summon at will. Part of its allure and impact is caused by the fact that it lies beyond our control. But there are also some important ways in which we can increase the likelihood of inspiration visiting us from time to time and of it driving us forward over the course of our lives.

We can seek out stimulating new experiences of the world, particularly ones we know might trigger a lift in our spirits. We can also seek to reflect more internally, attempting to better understand and articulate our motivations and the passions that make us feel most alive.

Perhaps most importantly, we can bring an engaging mindset that leaves us open, receptive and ready to be inspired. 'Life can be cruel and take many things away from you, but what it can never take is your power over the way you think,' Claire concludes. By choosing to be positive about life, to embrace possibilities and to look for learning, we can create the fertile conditions in our minds that make inspiration more likely to flourish.

In the coming chapters, we will look in more detail at each of the three elements that help to bring about the experience of inspiration. In this chapter, we have introduced them from the outside in – from triggers, to mindsets and then to motivations. To help maximize our insight, we will now look at things in the other direction, starting internally and moving externally:

- What are the key *internal motivations* that fuel your spirit and passion?

- How can you bring more *engaging mindsets* in the way you relate to yourself and the world around you?

- Which *external triggers* do you find most evocative?

By exploring the answers to these questions, your own potential sources of leadership inspiration should soon become clearer.

THE ALCHEMY OF INSPIRATION: IN SUMMARY...

- Inspiration takes place when three crucial elements come together for us in a unique and magical way:
  - The *triggers* we encounter in the external world – the situations, events and people we experience as we progress through our lives.
  - The *mindsets* we bring to engage with these experiences and relate them to our own selves.
  - The *motivations* we feel internally, especially the values, interests and talents we have most passion for.

- Leadership inspiration involves an uplifting sense of opportunity to make the most of ourselves as human beings and to maximize our positive impact on the people and the world around us.

- Because we exist in the context of *time*, we have the extraordinary opportunity to improve ourselves, to develop our capabilities and to increase our influence beyond ourselves as our lives progress.

- Although we cannot control exactly how and when we feel inspired, there are some important ways in which we can increase the likelihood of inspiration driving us forward over the course of our lives:

    ○ Reflecting internally to better understand and articulate our motivations and the passions that make us feel most alive.

    ○ Choosing to be positive about life, to embrace possibilities and to seek lifelong learning about ourselves.

    ○ Seeking out stimulating new experiences of the world, particularly ones we know can trigger a lift in our spirits.

REFLECTIONS 1: MY INSPIRATION LIFELINE

As you look back over your life to date, to what extent have you felt 'inspired'? Have there been phases when your motivation levels were higher than at other times?

To help you answer these questions, try charting your spirits using the map on the next page. Divide the bottom axis up into the key stages of your life – school, college, different jobs, etc. Then draw a line showing the relative level of inspiration you've felt over time. Here's an example of what it might look like.

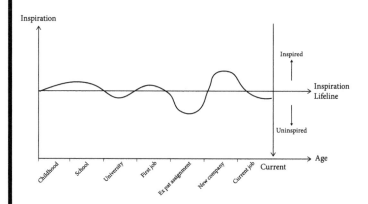

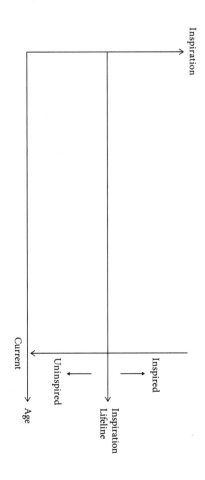

Having completed your Inspiration Lifeline, now have a go at capturing the reasons it looks the way it does.

When were you most inspired?   *What were the reasons?*

When were you least inspired?   *What were the reasons?*

We will return to explore what you can learn about yourself from your experience of life to date in the coming chapters.

WHAT YOU GET BY ACHIEVING YOUR GOALS
IS NOT AS IMPORTANT AS WHAT YOU
BECOME BY ACHIEVING YOUR GOALS.

HENRY DAVID THOREAU

2

DISCOVER	
1	The Alchemy of Inspiration
2	Internal Motivations
3	Engaging Mindsets
4	External Triggers

'After a long career in business, what has struck me most has been that when you get towards the top of the mountain, the view isn't quite what you were expecting.'

This is the curious perspective of Martin George, a businessman who has served on the senior leadership teams of companies such as British Airways, Bupa and Thorntons. One of his most recent roles has been as commercial director of the Post Office.

'I always had the ambition of being a main board director in a big publicly listed company and, if I'm honest, I was very motivated by the status symbols, profile and influence that I thought would come with it,' he admits. 'But now that I've got there, I've felt a strong sense of: "Is this it?" I recognize that I'm in a very fortunate position to enjoy many of those material benefits, but they certainly haven't brought me the fulfilment I expected.'

In reality, Martin has found his greatest rewards have arisen from other, less tangible sources. 'My deepest satisfaction has come in much more spiritual and emotional areas. When I've felt really joyful and inspired, it's usually been a consequence of human interaction – being with somebody, having an experience with somebody, being able to help someone out.'

'I've got a very different perspective now on what it means to reach the top of the mountain. In fact in some ways I've got a different view on the kind of mountain that's worth climbing in the first place,' Martin confesses. 'In Maslow's terms, the top of the mountain actually comes when you achieve that inner peace, being at one with yourself and your values.'

The motivation of human beings

Martin refers of course to Abraham Maslow's seminal work to define a hierarchy of human needs. Maslow suggested that although people's conscious desires may differ in a myriad of ways, the fundamental drivers of human behaviour are much less variable.

He went on to rank a core group of needs in terms of their 'prepotency', starting with our *physiological* needs and moving on to *safety, social, esteem* and *self-actualization*. He argued that our first priority is to meet needs at the bottom of the hierarchy. As this is achieved, our focus then shifts progressively to needs that are activated at the next level up.

Surprisingly though, despite its fame, there is little empirical substantiation for Maslow's original theory. His ideas undoubtedly helped transform the way we think about human motivation. But in recent years, other researchers have proposed modifications to the core needs he defined and even challenged the principle that we progress sequentially up a need hierarchy.

Of particular importance is the groundbreaking research pioneered by two psychologists called Richard Ryan and Edward Deci. Over thirty years ago, they set out to initiate a paradigm shift in the way human motivation is studied. Instead of focusing on how our behaviour can be influenced and controlled *from the outside*, their interest has centred on what drives people's motivation *from within*. The result is an extensive body of research integrated into what is now termed *self-determination theory*.

As complex as our drives as human beings may be, the way we are motivated to behave is similar to even the most basic living organisms in one key respect. At a fundamental biological level, we are all programmed to do things which promote our survival and well-being by *approaching* things in our environment that are in our interest and *avoiding* things that aren't.

Ryan and Deci argue that our evolution has resulted in us possessing a number of *basic needs* that are universally essential for our growth, integrity and well-being. Some of these are physiological – our requirement for food, water, oxygen and physical safety. In addition, though, there are some core psychological needs that must also be met if we are to thrive as individuals. There is no hierarchical ranking between them – they must all be met together if we are to flourish, as is the case with our basic physiological needs.

In order to understand these psychological needs, Ryan and Deci's research has explored in great depth why individuals feel energetic, alive and invigorated in some situations and not in others. They describe this state as one of *subjective vitality* and have shown it occurs when a distinctive type of motivation is present.

They make a critical distinction between *intrinsic* motivation, which refers to doing something because it is inherently rewarding, and *extrinsic* motivation, which involves doing something because it leads on to a separate desirable outcome. They have found that our spirit as human beings comes alive when our motivation is intrinsic – when we feel *self-determined* and we can express freely our human nature to explore, learn and engage with others.

Deci and Ryan go on to suggest that many of our extrinsic motivations – for example, the desire for wealth, social approval or power – are often driven by substitute or compensatory motives when our basic intrinsic needs are being frustrated. In some instances, the evidence even suggests that meeting our extrinsic goals can *undermine* our intrinsic aspirations.

The shortfalls of extrinsic motivations

Martin George is not alone in having been attracted by the financial rewards, the social status and the influence that come with a senior role. However, these motivations are *extrinsic* in nature. We end up enjoying the rewards *as a result* of our work as leaders – they are not inherent in the actual work itself.

This helps explain why Martin is also not alone in discovering that a materialistic and egocentric approach to life is often a lot less fulfilling than expected. A growing body of research is showing that people are more likely to suffer from stress and burnout if they are motivated more by wealth and image than by other factors such as their own personal growth and their empathy, altruism and compassion for others.

It is not the case that extrinsic motivations are *by definition* less rewarding than intrinsic motivations. The issues arise when our behaviour is driven by extrinsic motivations that are not *internalized* and *integrated* with our basic human desire for autonomy and self-expression. For example, our vitality will suffer if we are doing a job because we feel we need to earn a high salary, but we do not fundamentally enjoy the work involved or believe in its value. It is the sense of choice or volition over what we are doing that makes such an important difference to our relative levels of engagement and fulfilment.

Martin recognizes that there is a dilemma involved in his extolling the virtues of this more enlightened perspective now that he has reached such a senior corporate position. 'It's complicated because I can imagine saying to younger people that it's not all about the money, and them saying back: "Well you can say that can't you, because you've already got some!"' he acknowledges. 'But I do think there's a risk we spend a large proportion of our lives striving for success measured by a set of criteria that prove to be, in some cases, misguided.'

Arianna Huffington is another high-profile example of someone who has come to a similar conclusion. In her revealing book *Thrive*, she explains how her excessive focus on money and power had left her feeling exhausted and out of control. She talks about the stress so many people are feeling caused by *over*busyness, *over*working and *over*connecting on social media, and *under*connecting with themselves and with one another.

Like Martin George, Huffington advocates the need to rethink our understanding of what it means to be successful. She suggests that, over the long term, money and power are like an unstable, two-legged stool. A third leg is required to provide greater balance, incorporating considerations such as one's personal well-being, wisdom, generosity and a sense of wonder at the world.

The power of intrinsic motivations

Ryan and Deci's work suggests that the path to experiencing more positive energy and direction in our lives depends upon us activating our *intrinsic* motivations. They have identified three basic psychological needs that are all fundamental to influencing our personal growth, integrity and wellness.

- *Autonomy:* the desire to have control over our lives and to act in harmony with our true selves
- *Competence:* the desire to experience a sense of mastery in performing tasks that matter to us
- *Relatedness:* the desire to interact, connect and experience caring relationships with others

It is these positive 'approach' motivations that help explain what makes us feel inspired. When they are activated together, we feel engaged, enthusiastic and boosted by a sense that we are making the most of ourselves as human beings. Interestingly, this state is closely aligned with the way Maslow originally defined self-actualization at the top of his need hierarchy: 'To become everything we are capable of becoming.' The difference is that there is now much more research evidence clarifying how this state can be reached in reality.

Further insights about the positive feelings we associate with intrinsic motivation are emerging in the field of neuroscience. Researchers point to a linkage between intrinsic motivation and a *seeking system* that seems to be hardwired into the brains of mammals. This system is believed to energize our exploratory engagement with the external environment, and the mental processes associated with our feelings of interest, curiosity, sensation-seeking and our search for higher meaning.

Central to the neurochemistry of our brain's seeking system is a neurotransmitter called dopamine. Not only does this hormone enable us to recognize potential rewards in the world around us, it also helps regulate our action to move towards them. Crucially, the release of dopamine is associated with feelings of enjoyment, love, exhilaration and heightened energy and motivation levels, which helps explain why our experience of intrinsic motivation feels so uplifting.

Intrinsic motivation in action

Jon Harding is an experienced HR leader who has held a variety of senior roles in companies such as Barclays, Intercontinental

Hotels Group and Diageo. His extensive involvement in leadership development and employee engagement over the years has made him a strong believer in the power of Ryan and Deci's ideas. 'This isn't just a nice theory,' he asserts. 'I've seen it so many times, not just in the work I've done with other leaders, but also in myself.'

'You feel inspired when your work actually matters and you feel that you're contributing to something larger than yourself,' he continues. 'It happens when you feel a sense of control over your own destiny and when you're doing things you love doing for their own sake. Inspiration comes when you get totally absorbed in your work because you're fascinated with the subject and you're challenged to solve, improve and get good at things. These are the things that propel people forward and make them feel fully alive.'

Jon has an interesting perspective on why leaders are so often apparently focused on financial rewards, rather than the potentially more inspirational dimensions of their work. 'Once you get to a certain point, it's not about the amount of money you earn. The issue is that people are constantly looking to prove themselves and it's what they earn *relative to others* that really matters to them. It's a sign of how much their organisation loves them.'

But Jon is clear that this orientation has some important downsides. 'I think what happens a lot of the time is that people lose any sense of why they are doing what they are doing. Work has just become a habit for them. They've chosen the corporate life and they just keep going. Ultimately, this leads to a level of unhappiness for many of them, a lack of fulfilment and sometimes a lot of anxiety.'

The drivers of leadership inspiration

One of the goals of my own research has been to translate these insights in a way that is more accessible for leaders personally. The result is the framework in Figure 2 showing the Drivers of Leadership Inspiration.

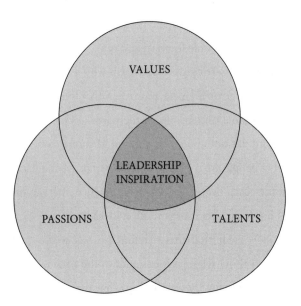

FIGURE 2 *The Drivers of Leadership Inspiration.*

As we proceed on our journey through time, there are three very practical ways in which we can seek to activate our intrinsic motivations and thereby drive our chances of discovering leadership inspiration:

- Follow our *passions*, by getting involved in work that we love and find most fascinating
- Apply our *talents*, by playing to our strengths and stretching our personal qualities and capabilities
- Live our *values*, by upholding the principles we believe in and care about most deeply

My research suggests that leaders feel inspired when these three conditions are present together in their thoughts, feelings and activities. This finding can be explained by the fact that each plays a significant role in helping us fulfil our three basic psychological needs.

When we play to our *passions*, we exploit our freedom to do the things that we find intrinsically most stimulating and enjoyable (autonomy). We also have the opportunity to strengthen our expertise in these activities (competence) and to build our connections with other like-minded people based on our shared interests (relatedness).

When we utilize our *talents*, we make the most of our personal capabilities and aptitudes (competence). We also exert influence and control over our personal circumstances (autonomy) and build our self-confidence in engaging with others (relatedness).

When we promote our *values*, we establish the basis for our relationships and our influence on other people (relatedness). In so doing, we also express a core part of our self-identity (autonomy) and enhance our personal qualities and behaviours in support of the principles we believe in (competence).

Discovering inspiration in practice

To bring these concepts to life, let us go back to Martin George and explore where he draws his inspiration from as a leader today.

Passions

'I love the idea of being the source of change and a source of ideas within the business. I love creating the energy needed to help make things happen,' Martin declares. 'For me, this is what leadership is all about. I love the thought that you can walk into a meeting and help people come out with a better outcome, or the same outcome but with more enthusiasm behind it.'

Martin is also very passionate about the role he plays in supporting the development of the people around him. 'As I've got older, I've found it incredibly inspiring to see people grow and to know that I've played a small part in helping them on their way', he continues. 'That probably gives me a bigger reward than seeing the profits going from X to Y, or the customer numbers going from A to B. Because if you're helping everyone to be the best they can be, everyone feels fulfilled personally and you're also building the capacity for the whole organization to succeed in the future.'

Talents

'When I started out in business, I think there was a sense that you worked out what your strengths and weaknesses were and then focused all your attention on sorting out your weaknesses', Martin reflects. 'I've become increasingly conscious that, as long as your weaknesses aren't terminal, you need to focus more on playing to your strengths. I'm not past caring about my weaknesses, but I try to be overt about them and address them in the way I build my team around me.'

What are the most important talents that Martin sees in himself? 'I try to bring positive energy and confidence to a team, and I also try to make sure people remain both customer-focused and commercial', he shares. 'At the heart of it, I guess it's about me being able to create a drum beat, creating an energy, making things happen and hopefully bringing a bit of fun along the way.'

Values

Martin has a clear sense of the values that underpin the way he approaches his work and his life more generally. 'I believe everybody starts equal and should be given equal opportunity, and I think the Post Office exhibits that really well,' he explains. 'I would also only ever work for a business that genuinely cares about its customers and does all it can to offer real value, rather than ripping them off in any way. These things really matter to me.'

Martin also believes strongly in the importance of being conscientious. 'It's something I learned from my dad who worked unbelievably hard, but for not a lot of money. He wanted me to work as hard as him, but to have a better life. I guess that's one of the reasons for my materialistic motivation, because that's what I used to think striving for a better life meant.'

Taking all these elements together, it is clear that Martin George now has a very different perspective on his purpose as a leader. He has an important desire to work for a company that provides products or services that make a real difference to people. 'At Bupa, we used to talk about doing well by doing good, because our commercial success was founded upon our role in helping people live longer, healthier, happier lives,' Martin recalls.

'At the Post Office, the emphasis is on the need to be a commercial business with a strong social purpose. That mission is to support the 11,500 communities in which its branches exist, by helping the people that live in them get the important things in life done – things like getting hold of travel money, passports, driving licences, road tax, savings policies and so on.'

Martin's orientation has changed at a personal level too. 'If there is one unifying theme for where I get my inspiration from today, I guess it's in the role I play inspiring people to focus on our customers, so that our business becomes more successful. It's joining up those three things – people, customers and commerciality – that's ultimately what my leadership is about.'

The insights of a young leader

I recently had the privilege of serving on The Marketing Society's judging panel for the UK's Young Marketing Leader of the Year. The winner we chose was a Norwegian called Anne-Lise Johnsen for the excellent job she has done as Youth Product Manager for Arsenal Football Club (as a Liverpool fan myself this wasn't an easy decision, but credit where credit's due!).

Anne-Lise joined Arsenal when she was just twenty-six, and over the past four years, she has helped build their Junior Gunners club into one of the largest football youth membership schemes in the world. However, Anne-Lise's awareness and presence as a leader was at least as impressive as the commercial results she has achieved.

In many of my interviews with older leaders, concerns have been expressed about how difficult it can be for young people to discover a true sense of their passions, talents and values when their experience of life is relatively limited. My encounter with Anne-Lise helped put many of those fears to rest.

'I've always been a creative person – I loved doing arts and crafts when I was younger,' Anne-Lise begins. 'But I'm also quite analytical – I like logical reasoning; I like processes and planning. So my dad suggested to me that I start studying marketing as an elective when I was fifteen. I responded really well to it and enjoyed the blend of the different ways of thinking.'

'I was also really into sports and loved playing football,' she continues. 'I never thought of it as a career route, but then when I was seventeen I got badly injured. It was then I began wondering whether I could find a way to continue working with my passion, rather than just go on playing as a spare time activity.'

Anne-Lise went on to study for a master's degree in marketing management at Lancaster University and wrote her dissertation on sports marketing. Initially she struggled to get a job, but she managed to get a temporary role with graduate recruitment website Milkround, owned by News International. It was then that she saw a LinkedIn ad for the role at Arsenal.

'The headhunter told me initially that I wasn't qualified for it because I hadn't been down a traditional consumer goods training path,' she explains. 'But I made the point that the job involved youth marketing, which meant my digital background would be a real strength.'

'I think this gives an example of another of my strengths – my directness. I think it's come from when I was captain of my football and handball teams,' Anne-Lise reflects. 'I'm used to getting people going and believing in something. I have a lot of time for building relationships, but I also tend to talk straight to the point.'

Anne-Lise has identified her four most important values, a consequence of her attending the well-respected Marketing Academy leadership development programme. 'The first is *honesty*. I've always been told to be an honest person, and I expect that of other people too. The second is *loyalty*. I'm very loyal if I'm treated right, and that transcends to my friends and relationships outside of work too. I also want to have *fun*, which is the reason I haven't gone down certain career routes. And finally there's *ambition*. I'm ambitious at work and also in my personal life – I'm one of those people who wants to go for it all!'

'The biggest benefit of knowing my values has been to build my self-confidence and to help me feel a greater degree of comfort in myself,' Anne-Lise discloses. 'I've certainly felt very inspired. The job at Arsenal really has been my dream job. I've got to work in two areas I love – sport and youth. I'm doing something I enjoy and that I'm becoming quite good at – marketing. And it's been a tough but exciting challenge, getting people in the club to see the potential of the youth scheme and to get them all engaged behind making it a success.'

In conclusion, what advice would Anne-Lise give to other young people trying to find their way in life? 'In some shape or form, follow your passion. Lots of people don't do so and say it's probably not possible, but I don't agree. If you love music – find a way of working in it. You don't have to be a musician. If you love animals – find a way of working with them. Look at what really drives you. What will get you out of bed every day?'

Anne-Lise Johnsen's story proves that, even at a young age, it is possible to get in touch with our intrinsic motivations and use them to guide our career choices. She appears to be putting into practice the advice of Martin George and Arianna Huffington, by placing greater emphasis on these considerations as she plans her journey through time.

How conscious are you of *your* intrinsic motivations? The next set of reflective questions are designed to help you consider the internal drivers of your own leadership inspiration.

INTERNAL MOTIVATIONS: IN SUMMARY...

- Human beings have a few basic needs that are universally essential for our growth, integrity and well-being over time, but evidence now indicates that these are not activated in a hierarchy as Maslow famously proposed.

- Our spirit as human beings comes alive when our motivation is intrinsic rather than extrinsic, when we feel self-determined and when we can express freely our inherent human desire to explore, learn and engage with others.

- Some leaders are motivated by *extrinsic* factors such as money, status and power, but an egocentric and materialistic approach to life is often a lot less fulfilling than expected.

- A greater sense of subjective vitality arises when three basic psychological needs are satisfied:

  ○ *Autonomy*: the desire to have control over our lives and to act in harmony with our true selves.

  ○ *Competence*: the desire to experience a sense of mastery in performing tasks that matter to us.

  ○ *Relatedness*: the desire to interact, connect and experience caring relationships with others.

- There are three practical ways in which we can seek to activate our intrinsic motivations and thereby drive our chances of discovering leadership inspiration:

  ○ Follow our *passions*, by getting involved in work that we love and find most interesting

  ○ Apply our *talents*, by playing to our strengths and finding ways to stretch our personal qualities and capabilities

  ○ Live our *values*, by upholding the principles we believe in and care about most deeply

- It is possible to live a more inspired life by striking a better balance between our extrinsic and intrinsic motivations, even during the early stages of our careers.

REFLECTIONS 2: MY MOTIVATIONS

To become more conscious of your own intrinsic motivations, have a look back at your Inspiration Lifeline in the last chapter as you reflect on the following questions.

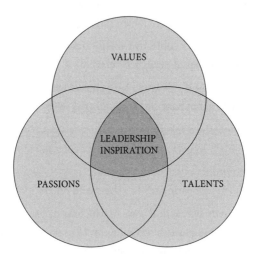

Passions*: What are the activities you find most fascinating and enjoyable?*

Talents: *What are the key personal capabilities and aptitudes that you want to make the most of?*

Values: *What are the core values you believe in and want to stand for in life?*

How are your answers to these questions reflected in the leadership role you play currently?

What else is motivating you to do the job you do today?

How can you strike a better balance between your extrinsic and intrinsic motivations (i.e. wealth, status and power versus passions, talents and values)?

We will use these thoughts about the drivers of your leadership inspiration to help you define your personal purpose as a leader in Chapter 6.

I CAN COMPLAIN BECAUSE
ROSE BUSHES HAVE THORNS,
OR I CAN REJOICE BECAUSE
THORN BUSHES HAVE ROSES.

J. KENFIELD MORLEY

3

DISCOVER	
1	The Alchemy of Inspiration
2	Internal Motivations
3	Engaging Mindsets
4	External Triggers

In April 2015, a remarkable meeting took place between two of the world's great spiritual leaders – the Dalai Lama and Archbishop Desmond Tutu. The purpose was to spend a week together exploring how we as human beings can find greater joy in our lives. With both men now in their eighties, they each brought a lifetime of extraordinary worldly and spiritual experience to the conversation.

An account of their discussion is written up beautifully in *The Book of Joy* by Douglas Abrams. At the heart of the ideas they shared is one key thought – that the extent to which we experience joy or suffering in our life is determined in large part by our own mindsets. 'It simply depends on the attitudes, the perspectives and the reactions we bring to situations and to our relationships with other people,' the Dalai Lama explains.

This brings us to the second element that enables the alchemy of inspiration. Our mindsets are the ways in which we think about ourselves and interpret the world around us.

In the last chapter, we considered how our internal motivations determine what we ultimately find most appealing and rewarding. However, the assumptions we make and the stories we formulate in our minds also play a crucial role in influencing the way we engage with the people, events and circumstances we encounter.

By *choosing* the perspectives we bring, rather than letting them happen by default, we have an important opportunity to shape our experience of life so that it connects with our motivations in more positive and inspiring ways.

A life in exile

The Dalai Lama's personal story provides a great example. Over sixty years ago, in 1950, he was plunged into politics at the age of just fifteen following the invasion of Tibet by China. The ruler of his country's six million people, he did his best to negotiate a peaceful solution with the Chinese for nine years. Eventually, though, he was forced into exile and since 1959 he has been living over the border in Northern India as a political refugee.

The way the Dalai Lama has handled this situation over the years has become legendary. 'If you look from one angle, you feel: "Oh how bad, how sad,"' he observes. 'But if you look from another angle at that same tragedy, that same event, you see that it gives me new opportunities. So, it's wonderful.'

Rather than despairing at the loss of his homeland, he has found the inspiration to move beyond his previously cloistered environment, to broaden his experience and play a more influential leadership role on the world stage.

Desmond Tutu is no stranger to oppression and persecution himself, having been through the apartheid era in South Africa. His reflections on the lessons we can draw from the Dalai Lama's experience are typically insightful. He acknowledges the extreme nature of Tibet's plight, but makes the point that pain and frustration are inevitable in all our lives to some extent. The challenge is not to try and escape these difficulties, but to find the strength within ourselves to *accept* the fact that they are happening to us, just as the Dalai Lama himself managed to do.

Rather than occupying our minds by punishing ourselves, or railing against the injustice of our situation, we can each turn our attention instead to what Archbishop Tutu sees as the most important question – how can we use this as something *positive*?

The other central theme to emerge from their week of discussion was the importance of our generosity and compassion for others as a source of our own joy and fulfilment. 'Materialistic values cannot give us peace of mind, so we really need to focus on our inner values, our true humanity,' advises the Dalai Lama.

The two leaders are united in seeing a paradox in the way human beings are motivated, just as we highlighted in the previous chapter. They point to the fact that people become selfish with a view to maximizing their own happiness and well-being. Yet the true path to that goal actually involves us embracing our need for *relatedness*, and being at least as concerned for other people's happiness and well-being as for our own. Desmond Tutu concludes, 'Ultimately our greatest joy is when we do good for others.'

The impact of mindsets

It may not be surprising to hear this kind of altruistic point of view being expressed by two such eminent religious leaders. However, there is growing scientific evidence to support their apparent wisdom.

A great deal more psychological research has been done into the drivers of human happiness generally, than of inspiration specifically. Nevertheless, the findings certainly help to enhance our understanding of the role mindsets play in influencing the emotional and spiritual rewards we can obtain from life.

Until recently, psychologists believed that people's genetic make-up meant they have a 'set point' that determines the level of happiness they typically experience over the course of their lives. Some people are lucky enough to have higher set points than others, which leads them to have a generally happier disposition. Our happiness levels can increase or decrease versus our personal set point as our circumstances change, but they soon return to our set level once we become accustomed to any new situation.

However, new research by a psychologist at the University of California called Sonja Lyubomirsky has challenged this theory. She has found that only 50 per cent of people's happiness is determined by their set point. People's life circumstances explain a further 10 per cent – whether they are healthy or unhealthy, rich or poor, loved or unloved, fat or thin, etc. The remaining 40 per cent is influenced by people's attitudes and behaviour and is therefore more within their own control.

Lyubomirsky emphasizes three factors we can all influence that have a significant impact on our potential levels of happiness. The first is to bring an attitude of gratitude and appreciation for all the good things in our lives. The second is our ability to reframe our experiences in positive ways, finding benefits and opportunities rather than dwelling on negative thoughts and fears. The third is simply to be kind and generous to others.

These findings provide compelling scientific justification for the exhortations of the Dalai Lama and Archbishop Tutu. The exciting implication is that by choosing to think in these positive and less self-orientated ways, we all have the power to enhance our subjective experience of life.

It is important to point out a couple of catches though. First, both the psychologists and the spiritual leaders agree that focusing our efforts on trying to be happy or joyful as ends in themselves will be counter-productive. These feelings are best seen as by-products of the genuine, compassionate attitudes we have highlighted. As we shall discover later, it is safe to infer that the same is true of inspiration.

Second, achieving and applying these mindsets in practice is not easy. It often requires tremendous fortitude and courage, as the experiences over the years of both the Dalai Lama and Desmond Tutu have demonstrated so admirably.

All the same, despite these caveats, the potential spiritual rewards available to us from engaging in life with the appropriate mindsets are immense. With an open, positive and generous attitude, we have an opportunity to discover inspiration in even the most challenging situations.

The relationship with creative inspiration

There is a further significant dimension to the kind of mindset that fosters leadership inspiration. And if I am honest, it is one that I unwittingly set out to ignore when I first began my research work.

I took a decision, early in the project, not to broaden the scope of the investigation to include *creative* inspiration. This was driven partly by a desire to keep the project focused and manageable, but also by a belief that this was a distinct type of inspiration with very different outcomes.

As we have learned already, *leadership* inspiration relates to our desire to make the most of ourselves and to drive positive change in the world around us. *Creative* inspiration is more concerned with experiencing the breakthrough or 'aha' moments that lead to the generation of novel ideas. My initial perspective was that these two forms of inspiration were entirely distinct, with no inter-relationship.

Without wishing to downplay some very real differences between them, the more I have learned, the more I have come to appreciate that many of the *mindsets* that help foster each type of inspiration are actually very similar. This realization has been accompanied by a growing recognition of the role that creativity plays in the art of leadership.

Inspired leaders possess the imagination to see new, exciting possibilities in the future. Their passionate curiosity helps them make insightful connections that other people have not yet seen or envisaged. They see problems merely as creative briefs, requiring resolution through positive and lateral thought. They have the humility to value the ideas, efforts and activities of other people at least as much as they do their own. And they paint pictures and tell stories in ways that inspire other people to want to join them on their journeys.

Bringing stories to life

The similarities in the ways of thinking that help people discover both creative and leadership inspiration are illustrated vividly by the perspectives and experiences of a creative leader called Juliette Howell.

Juliette is a film and television executive who recently co-founded the independent House Productions company with her business partner, Tessa Ross. Her production credits include multi-Oscar-winning *Slumdog Millionaire* and BAFTA winners *Billy Elliott*, *Last King of Scotland*, *Shameless, Sex Traffic, Birdsong* and *London Spy*. Juliette began her broadcasting career in the drama department at the BBC, before moving on to Channel 4 and Film Four, where she was a drama commissioner. Most recently she was head of television at Working Title Films.

'I suppose I was driven originally by a sense that I wanted to tell stories and to work with writers in the realm of fiction,' Juliette recalls. 'As a child I was an avid reader and I became more and more curious about the mechanics of story-telling.'

'It wasn't about telling my own stories particularly – I had more of an appetite for the stories of others,' she continues. 'I have always been fascinated by people and how their life experiences have influenced their differing viewpoints on the world. I now see my job as giving them a voice and helping them shape their stories to share with others in the best possible form.'

Juliette has an interesting view on the way that creative inspiration works in this context. 'In my experience, it's rarely about big light bulb moments where everything suddenly changes. It's more granular than that, with every production made up of a whole series of incremental creative steps which ultimately add up to something special.'

As an example, Juliette recalls how the concept for a recent BBC show emerged. 'It began in a conversation where we were riffing about whether you can ever truly know your partner. What kind of secrets might there be in a relationship? Could that be the basis for a drama? What kind of characters might be involved? Soon afterwards, a big story broke in the news and that gave us an angle, a way of developing the relationship we'd been considering. It's all about making these little connections, joining up your experiences and your ideas and bouncing them around with the people you're working with.'

The bulk of Juliette's work has been in television where her role as an executive producer is pivotal in the developmental process. 'Essentially, you're the person who pulls everything together,' Juliette explains. 'You might read a book and think: "This would make a wonderful piece of television – I wonder who could adapt it?" You then commission a writer you love and support them as they write the screenplay. You search for a broadcaster, find the finances and pull the director and the rest of the production team together. You literally guide it through from start to finish. In a way, each television production is like a little company and you are the person leading that company.'

Juliette soon discovered that this leadership aspect within the job was very important to her own motivation and fulfilment. 'Film-making is such a collaborative process. If you don't have some control over the team, with a voice at every stage, the little seed of an idea you started with can easily morph in a direction you hadn't imagined. Sometimes that can be a wonderful revelation, but it can also be very frustrating if the potential of the idea ends up not being realized. An idea needs to be championed, sometimes sensitively and sometimes more bullishly. If you're leading the process, you have the influence to play the role that's required.'

Being a creative leader

What kind of mindsets does Juliette consider best support her leadership of the creative process? 'This is all about being part of a team, so communication between people is absolutely key,' she begins. 'If you go into it with too big an ego, you quickly make it very difficult for people to share their thoughts and feelings or to drill down within themselves to expose the truth and humanity you are looking for in a piece. You end up closing down interesting possibilities that you may not have been able to imagine yourself.'

'I also believe very strongly in transparency and openness,' she continues. 'Those are two of the qualities that I think are fundamental to me being able to do my job, both creatively and as a leader. In a business which is all about translating the stories in people's heads, you have to really listen and appreciate their views without judging them. The same principles apply if you want to encourage that same trust and sensibility within your own team too.'

Juliette also emphasizes the value of exploring and broadening one's own personal experience of the world. 'Curiosity is hugely important. So many of the ideas that excite us come from an article we happen to read, or a blog or a conversation. Hearing people who have dissimilar experiences and views can be so stimulating, but you have to be very careful not to impose your own way of thinking or shape what they say by asking them leading questions.'

'It's about being happy to put yourself outside your comfort zone,' she continues. 'You have to dismiss the idea that you might be judged and take yourself into places that are unfamiliar, and sometimes even dangerous! I am always asking the team: "What are the worlds we have never seen on our TV screens? Who are the people we have never met and who have never had a voice?" You won't answer these questions by staying within your own bubble. You have to put yourself in situations where you cannot predict the outcome.'

Juliette concludes by reinforcing the point we explored earlier about the importance of a positive mindset, especially when facing challenging situations. 'A spirit of positivity is absolutely vital,' she asserts. 'We recently won a big commission for a new television show, our first significant production as a new company. It was a huge achievement and the team had worked incredibly hard for six months to pull it off. When we heard the news, it was important for me to go and congratulate them.'

'However, what they didn't know was that the budget being made available was only about half what we had expected,' Juliette discloses. 'In the back of my mind, I wasn't even sure we would be able to make the production, but I knew that this was not the moment to share that information. Instead, you have to think to yourself: "Okay, let's look at this as a positive challenge. Who can we go to for the rest of the money? How do we enthuse them about the project? How might that make the possibilities even bigger and better?"'

Choosing our mindset

In line with our findings in Chapter 2, Juliette Howell's inspiration as a leader is driven by her *passion* for telling people's stories, her *talent* for their dramatic and compelling expression and her belief in *values* such as truth, openness and collaboration. But it is also fostered by a variety of mindsets that determine how she engages with the world and all the potential inspirational triggers it contains.

The mindsets that Juliette advocates are similar in many ways to those espoused earlier by the Dalai Lama, Desmond Tutu and Sonja Lyubomirsky: accepting the reality of challenging situations and looking to turn them into positive opportunities;

a sense of humility and generosity in the way we behave towards others; a desire to explore and to learn, rather than to judge others and ourselves; and a sense of fascination and gratitude for all the wonders that the world has to offer.

These are the mindsets that will increase our chances of discovering personal inspiration, both creatively and as leaders. The two types of inspiration remain very different in some ways, but Juliette's experience shows that both can flourish alongside each other if we bring the right mental models and approaches. The big question is, how do we cultivate our ability to think in these more constructive ways in practice?

I probed on this issue with Juliette herself to learn how she seeks to manage her perspective as events unfold. 'Personally, I have found my relationship with my business partner, Tessa Ross, very important here. Being open about our fears and anxieties, talking things through, sharing in the responsibility – I have found all these things incredibly valuable. Working out between us the best way to think about something has helped us to bring that mindset in the way we then communicate with our broader team.'

'I also think you have to carve out time for yourself,' Juliette reflects. 'The job is so busy and so sociable, I know I sometimes just need some quiet thinking time. To some people that might sound a bit pretentious, but it's really not – it's vital.'

On this point, Juliette's experience mirrors that of many of the leaders I have spoken to. It is only by finding the time and space to think about ourselves and our leadership that we are able to strengthen our self-awareness as leaders. Stepping back from the heat of the action enables us to reflect and build a deeper understanding of what is really shaping our thinking and driving our behaviour.

The self-insight that results is critical if we are to achieve the consciousness necessary to change the mindsets we bring to different situations. By recognizing our default reactions as they occur, in the moment, we can then begin to choose different perspectives that enable us to interpret what is going on around us in more helpful ways.

The most experienced and successful leaders sometimes even progress to the point where they crystalize the philosophy they bring to their leadership in some key tenets or principles. These are constructed based on the experiences they have been through and are used to guide the mindsets they bring as they encounter new and unfamiliar situations.

A caring leader

Nihal Kaviratne CBE has eyes that are wise, kind, but also slightly mischievous. They have the disconcerting effect of leaving you never quite sure whether he's about to say something extremely astute or wonderfully funny!

Nihal is Indian by birth and had a long and illustrious career with Unilever. Named by Forbes India as one of the five best leaders to have on your board, he now serves as a non-executive director for many top companies. He is also the founder of St Jude's, a burgeoning charity providing shelter and care for street children undergoing cancer treatment in India.

'One always has to be careful to avoid clichés, but in my view being a true leader ultimately boils down to being someone who cares,' states Nihal. 'You care about the people you lead and you care about the things they care about – that's where the relationship begins.'

Nihal has a profound belief in the importance of relationships, owing in part to the painful experience of his parents divorcing when he was young. 'I never wanted to see again the severing of joyful relationships in any sphere of my life, be that at work, in marriage or in my friendships,' he explains.

This commitment was put to the test soon after he had met and fallen in love with a girl called Shyama. Nihal was at university in India in the mid-1960s when he had the opportunity to move to the United States with the offer of a scholarship from Harvard University. Instead, he made the choice to stay back in India to nurture his relationship with Shyama and their subsequent marriage remains as strong today as ever.

A set of leadership beliefs

'As your experience of life builds over the years, I think you begin to develop your own belief set,' Nihal suggests. He goes on to list three principles that have helped give clarity and inspiration to his own approach as a leader. The first he describes as an *unrelenting quest for truth.*

'We need to recognize that the boundaries of what we know are merely the boundaries of what we don't know, so you have to keep pushing those boundaries further all the time,' he argues. 'It doesn't mean that you don't need to take decisions based on the best information you have available at certain points in time, but it's vital to remain curious and to always keep searching for learning.'

We will return to examine the significance of a learning mindset in more detail in Chapter 8, taking into account the important insights of a psychologist called Carol Dweck. For now though, Nihal goes on to recall an important moment of learning in his own development as a leader.

'In the early years of my career, I thought it was all-important to know the *answers* to everything. If I didn't, I felt insecure, unprepared and vulnerable to being found out,' he admits. 'The moment when I became more of a leader was when I realized it was more important to be asking the right *questions*.'

'So often, we get caught up in a very blinkered view of things,' he continues. 'I feel an important responsibility to help people open their minds and make sure we've examined things properly. I always force myself to ask the question: "Is this part of a bigger picture that we should be aware of"?'

Nihal's second belief is that leaders must have the humility to *take responsibility for things in a causal sense*, particularly when something goes wrong. 'As a leader you have to be prepared to say: "I made a mistake. I took a calculated risk, but it's not worked and the responsibility is mine." It's amazing when you do it – everyone in the business stops running for cover and starts coming together to try and find a solution!'

Finally, Nihal advocates *delayed gratification*. 'What do I mean by that? It's about not going for the low-hanging fruit. Low-hanging fruit is for the goats! A leader must concern himself with the high-hanging fruit – the difficult jobs with the biggest risks, but also the biggest rewards.'

'I find this mindset useful in guiding every aspect of behaviour,' he observes. 'When you look at your inbox – deal with the tough messages first. In a meeting – sort out the difficult issues early on the agenda. It might make life less easy in the short term, but the rewards in the future make the sacrifices worthwhile.'

Mindsets to avoid

The mindsets advocated by Nihal Kaviratne endorse once again many of those introduced earlier in the chapter. However, Nihal goes one step further by highlighting three mindsets that are *least* likely to serve a leader well, in terms of either their own inspiration or that of the people they lead. 'The first is *arrogance*. It is one of the paradoxes of being an effective leader – you have to be self-confident, but you also need to have humility. The minute you start getting too proud or arrogant, you stop searching for the truth.'

'The second pitfall is an unwillingness to listen to others. You can be a star and rise up to positions of leadership, but if you're not a good listener you run the risk of becoming a diva, not a leader!' Nihal exclaims.

'The final mindset to avoid at all costs is stubbornness – holding your ground whatever the situation. A leader needs to be open-minded and sometimes you need the strength to bend like the willow, not to remain steadfast like the oak.'

Mindsets are a crucial element in the alchemy of leadership inspiration because they provide the interface between our inner life and the external world in which we live. They are grounded in our deepest personal motivations, character traits and experiences. But they are not fixed and we have the opportunity both to deepen our understanding of ourselves and to broaden our understanding of the world as time goes by.

As we have just heard, part of this process of self-development is made possible by our own internal reflection. However, a large part will be influenced by the stimulus we receive in the outside world. It is to the triggers of inspiration that we can encounter there that we will now turn our attention.

ENGAGING MINDSETS: IN SUMMARY...

- Our mindsets are the ways in which we think about ourselves and interpret the world around us.

- By choosing the perspectives we bring, rather than letting them exist by default, we have an important opportunity to shape our experience of life in more positive and inspiring ways.

- Some of the mindsets that can help increase our chances of experiencing happiness, joy and inspiration in our lives include the following:

  - Accepting ourselves for who we are and the reality of the situations we find ourselves in.

  - Looking for the positive benefits and opportunities in even the most difficult circumstances.

- ○ Being conscious of and grateful for the good things in our lives.

- ○ Being compassionate, kind and generous to other people.

- ○ Putting ourselves out of our comfort zone to experience the full diversity of the world we live in.

- ○ Being curious and looking to learn from everything we do.

- ○ Balancing our self-confidence and humility in equal measure.

- ○ Delaying our gratification by leaving the low-hanging fruit to the goats!

- Giving ourselves the time and space for self-reflection plays a crucial role in strengthening our self-awareness and development as leaders.

- Defining our own inspiring set of leadership beliefs or principles can help guide our mindsets when we encounter new and unfamiliar situations.

REFLECTIONS 3: MY MINDSETS

Have a go at assessing your own mindsets by using the scale below as thoughtfully and honestly as possible.

I feel unhappy with who I am and the life I lead	1 2 3 4 5 6 7	*I feel happy with who I am and the life I lead*
I tend to see problems rather than opportunities	1 2 3 4 5 6 7	*I tend to see opportunities rather than problems*
I feel resentful about the bad things in my life	1 2 3 4 5 6 7	*I feel grateful for the good things in my life*
My main focus is on my own self-interest	1 2 3 4 5 6 7	*I actively try to be kind and generous to other people*
I tend to stick with what and who I know	1 2 3 4 5 6 7	*I always seek out new experiences and relationships*
I am most interested in succeeding	1 2 3 4 5 6 7	*I am most interested in learning*
I am proud	1 2 3 4 5 6 7	*I am humble*
I tend to avoid difficult challenges	1 2 3 4 5 6 7	*I try to seek out difficult challenges*

What single shift in mindset would have the biggest impact on your chances of discovering more inspiration as a leader?

What kind of situations are you likely to face where this different mindset will be important?

What can you tell yourself when these moments arise to help you reframe your perspective in a more helpful and positive manner?

PEOPLE WILL FORGET WHAT YOU SAID,
PEOPLE WILL FORGET WHAT YOU DID,
BUT PEOPLE WILL NEVER FORGET
HOW YOU MADE THEM FEEL.

MAYA ANGELOU

4

DISCOVER	
1	The Alchemy of Inspiration
2	Internal Motivations
3	Engaging Mindsets
4	External Triggers

One afternoon, when she was ten years old, Phyll Opoku-Gyimah was out with a couple of her school friends in the London borough of Enfield. As they approached the town centre, they could see a demonstration taking place further down the road.

Phyll recollects being approached by a little old lady who began shepherding her off the street, giving her a warning as she did so. 'She told me: "You've got to be careful, you need to hide in this shop-front. Those people are coming down here and they don't like your sort."'

At the time, Phyll had no idea what the woman was talking about. But the demonstration in question was by the National Front, a prominent racist organization in Britain at the time. 'I can remember them coming past the shop, big guys with big boots, waving their swastika flags.'

The friends she was with were both white and one of them, a girl called Hayley, shared with Phyll her perspective on what was going on. 'She told me that her dad had told her these people actually had a point, because they don't like the country being "flooded."'

Phyll was brought up in North London and was the child of Ghanaian parents. 'My mother and father have inspired me no end,' she explains. 'This was the late 1970s, a time when the pubs used to have signs up saying: "No dogs, no Irish, no blacks." For two people to come into a country that wasn't theirs and face all the challenges of racism they've had to overcome; to take on menial jobs and show such resilience in protecting their kids and giving us a great start in life – that's been a real inspiration.'

'I think that moment in Enfield was the first time it really hit me. That was the beginning for me. In a roundabout way, it's motivated me to be the person I am.' Phyll is now the head of political campaigns and equality for the Public and Commercial Services Union, which represents over 200,000 government employees. She is also a co-founder of Black Pride, an organization set up in 2005 to represent the needs and aspirations of lesbian, gay, bisexual and transgender people of colour.

'I'm black, gay and female – that's a triple whammy of discrimination!' Phyll laughs. She has a warm and vivacious demeanour, but there are some serious convictions that underpin what she has chosen to do with her life. 'Anytime there is injustice, I just feel driven to do something about it,' she explains. 'I'm not an attention-grabber, but sometimes I think when people are not speaking up, you have to help give them a voice.'

Mentors and role models

Phyll started her career as a civil servant, working at the lowest grade in the Employment Centre. She moved on to the Job Centre, the Benefits Agency and then the Fraud Investigation Service. 'That didn't last long,' she jokes again. 'They told me I wasn't inconspicuous enough!'

As she progressed, there were two people who had a particular influence on her mindset and development. The first was Claire McGuckin, a lady Phyll worked for as a PA. 'She was very small, but so assertive and powerful,' Phyll recalls. 'She would sit in a meeting with ten men and say: "No, I don't agree, and these are my reasons – bang, bang, bang."'

'Claire always told me to stop making coffee for people and trying to please everyone. "Don't be so submissive!" she would say.' Phyll reflects on the nature of their relationship, 'I always wondered why she would send me away to do little tasks, giving me homework and things like that. Looking back now, I believe she saw something in me – something that I didn't see. By doing that for me, she put me in a place that has allowed me to lead the way I do now in the workplace.'

Stretching beyond her role at work to the broader community, the other person to have had a major influence on Phyll has been Linda Bellos, the well-known political campaigner for black and gay rights. 'She has been so inspirational to me, helping me navigate my way through life,' Phyll explains.

'I remember seeing her speak and feeling like a meek little mouse,' she continues. 'Oh my gosh, she was just fantastic. I would hear her talk about fighting for freedom, equality and justice and of making sure we're part of everything; that we're in the mainstream and not erased or forgotten. She spoke with such ease and confidence and she wasn't afraid to put her head above the parapet. I wanted to be up there speaking with her – not like her, *with* her.'

'Certain people in life show you how things can be done and give you the confidence that you can do things too,' Phyll concludes. 'Claire and Linda, those are the two people that did that for me … and here I am!'

The role of triggers

As our lives unfold over time, there are a plethora of influences that gradually, layer by layer, shape who we become as individuals. Most of our experiences are seemingly inconsequential, building our understanding of ourselves, the world and our place within it in minor, incremental ways.

However, as we look back over time, there are usually a small handful of outstanding events, circumstances or people we can identify that have played a defining role in our development as leaders. Phyll's memories of the moment in Enfield when she experienced aggressive racism for the first time, and her interactions with Claire McGuckin and Linda Bellos are good examples.

As we discovered in Chapter 1, these triggers are not inspirational in their own right. It is the unique meaning they have for us as individuals that makes them so influential. In the last couple of chapters we have seen that this depends on the mindsets we bring to interpret them and the underlying motivations they touch.

The two leading academic researchers on the topic of inspiration are Todd Thrash and Andrew Elliott. They emphasize the fact that inspiration is *evoked*, rather than willed or initiated by us. We get *inspired by* triggers, which play a critical role in stimulating the emergence of new ideas in our consciousness.

The other defining characteristics of inspiration are that these ideas *transcend* our everyday concerns and lift our thinking to matters of ultimate or existential importance. We also experience a positive-approach motivation that compels us to action. We are *inspired to* do and be certain things as a result.

The power of people

Of all the potential triggers for leadership inspiration, the *people* we encounter seem to be one of the most significant. As Phyll Opoku-Gyimah illustrated, our parents have a particularly important role to play as we form our values early in life, though these relationships are not always straightforward.

'My mother and father had extremely strict, religious beliefs,' Phyll explains. 'When I came out about my sexual orientation, that was a really hard journey to go through with them. But they have taught me so much about standing up for what I believe in and handling all the hurdles and fireballs that life can sometimes throw at you.'

Another extremely important influence on us as leaders is the individuals we work for over the course of our career. Many of the leaders I have interviewed talked about the inspiration they have derived from one or two of their bosses, especially those who have displayed human values they aspire to embody in their own lives and behaviour. (They have also often mentioned one or two who have done quite the opposite and motivated them in a different direction!). As Phyll indicated, a manager who shows they believe in us and helps mentor our development can have a transformational impact on our confidence and capability.

However, it is not only people in positions of authority who can inspire us. Many leaders speak of the rewards they get from meeting customers or people working at the frontline in their organizations. These contacts help connect them with the places where their leadership has the most tangible impact and value. Interactions with young people can also be very uplifting as they often bring such a fresh, creative and enthusiastic spirit to the work they do and the lives they lead.

Leaders can also benefit tremendously from the feedback they receive from their peers and colleagues, particularly when they learn more about the impact their presence and behaviour is having on the people they are leading. This self-insight is often enhanced further by individuals working with executive coaches or mentors. By providing a judicious blend of support and challenge, these specialists can play a critical role in helping leaders attain new levels of personal growth and performance.

Words of wisdom

Another stimulating source of human inspiration can be found by accessing the wisdom of previous generations, captured in the cultural forms of literature, music and poetry. As an example, Simon Lowden is the president for PepsiCo's global snacks business based in the United States. When he was 16, he was hugely disappointed to be turned down for a role in the air force. 'I was really very upset about this,' Simon remembers. 'So my dad gave me this poem by Rudyard Kipling called *If*, which is all about being stoical.'

The story behind the poem is poignant as Rudyard Kipling wrote the poem for his own son, who sadly died shortly afterwards in the First World War. 'The poem has had a very big impact on me as a leader and I've based a lot of my values and beliefs on it over the years,' reflects Simon. 'It talks about keeping your head when all those around you are losing theirs, about trusting yourself when others doubt you, and of walking with kings, but not losing the common touch.'

The poem is particularly significant for Simon just now, as his father is terminally ill with cancer. 'I'm seeing him quite a bit at the moment and he asked me recently whether I remember him giving me the poem. It gave me real pleasure to be able to tell him that I did and what a great source of inspiration it's been for me since.'

The impact of events and environment

Major milestones in our lives such as the loss of a parent can themselves be very powerful in triggering a re-evaluation of who we are and what we want to make of our lives. In one case, a teacher I spoke to described how it was the death of her mother that had helped prompt her decision to make the step up to become a school headmistress.

Other notable events such as big birthdays, a reunion with old friends or the loss of a job can all provoke us to think in new ways and awaken within us a new perspective on ourselves and our lives.

Extending beyond specific moments in time, there can also be longer phases in our lives when the circumstances in which we are living and working have a major impact on our spirits. The transformation that took place for Anne-Lise Johnsen when she joined Arsenal FC and for Juliette Howell when she became an executive producer are good examples. In both cases, they were inspired by having the opportunity to do what they love, to play to their strengths and to feel like they were doing something worthwhile.

There is an important lesson to be drawn from this. There is a risk that we see life as something that happens *to us*, rather than something we can proactively influence and shape. If we wait in the hope we might encounter people, circumstances or events that we find inspiring, we might be waiting a long time. In the spirit of the mindsets we explored in the last chapter, one of the most effective ways to bring more inspiration into our lives is to actively *seek out* triggers that we find inspirational.

Meeting interesting people, attending stimulating conferences, changing the kind of jobs we do or the companies we work for. These are not things we need to hope for – we can make them happen at any time.

One type of situation that seems especially potent as a trigger for leadership inspiration is when people face a demanding challenge. By seeking out circumstances we find testing, we can experience inspiring opportunities that stretch our personal capabilities and qualities to the limit.

Embracing challenging experiences

Niall FitzGerald KBE is an Irishman who confronted racism in a different way to Phyll Opoku-Gyimah, by taking on an expatriate assignment in South Africa during the apartheid years. At a time when most multinational organizations were withdrawing from the country in protest at its government's policies, Niall's company, Unilever, took the view that it could do more good by maintaining its presence. He was offered the local role of chief financial officer and soon went on to become the CEO of its South African food business.

'I was sent with a particular mission,' Niall recalls. 'We wanted to get our business to behave in a way which was consistent with Unilever's principles, despite the fact that in many cases this was against the law of the land.' There was obviously a considerable personal risk involved in this, so Niall only agreed to take the role on one condition. 'We established that if at any time in the first six months I wanted or needed to get out, I would just ask once and there would be no discussion – I'd be out. The irony was that five years later, when they rang to talk about me leaving, I didn't want to go!'

Niall remembers a seminal conversation with P. W. Botha, South Africa's prime minister at the time. 'He told me that if we broke the law, they'd put us in jail. I made it clear, in response, that a decision of that type would also have its consequences, and we left it at that.'

The Unilever management team proceeded to stand up for equal opportunities, refusing to implement segregation in its business operations. Although its activities in areas such as housing provision and toilet facilities were frequently challenged by local bureaucrats, there was never any concerted follow up by government officials.

'It proved to be one of the most inspiring and rewarding periods of my whole career,' Niall reflects. 'The most significant thing was that we had to be successful as a business at the same time as fighting for these principles. We outgrew our competitors, both top line and bottom line. That was what made us credible and encouraged more and more companies to emulate us. We certainly didn't get everything right, but there's no doubt, when I look back now, that we ended up having a huge social impact.'

The crucibles of leadership

Niall went on to become the chairman for the whole of Unilever's business between 1996 and 2004. He has since chaired a diverse range of organizations including Reuters, the British Museum, the Nelson Mandela Legacy Trust and, I'm delighted to say, my own company Brand Learning.

Given his extraordinary career success, Niall has an unexpected perspective on his sources of inspiration as a leader. 'If I look back over the moments when I derived the greatest inspiration, many of them have actually come when I had taken on a challenge and failed,' he admits. 'I guess it's ultimately human nature, but the sad fact is that it's only when you fail that you tend to examine what you've done properly. That's when you learn the most.'

A dramatic example came in 1994 when Unilever had to withdraw Persil Power, an innovative product line that was found to be damaging people's clothes. At the time, Niall was the head of Unilever's global detergents business and was widely assumed to be next in line for the role of the company's overall CEO.

'Up until that point in my career I hadn't made that many big mistakes, but this one was spectacular and also very public!' he recalls wryly. 'I went to the Board and explained we would have to mount a full-scale product withdrawal at a cost of about £350 million. I recognized that I would need to resign, but I asked them if I could stay on for about three months to see things through and help do what I could to rebuild the confidence of the team involved.'

Mike Perry, Unilever's chairman at the time, had other ideas. Niall recounts the ensuing conversation, 'He said to me: "You're not going anywhere. If you think we've invested £350 million in your education just for you to take it elsewhere – no way!"'

'I learned so much from that experience,' Niall confides. 'My style had been very much to lead from the front and to be in the trenches with people. But if I'm honest, I think part of the reason for that was that it had mattered too much to me to be popular. It's nice to be *respected*, but not necessarily *popular*. I realized it's more important to be driven by the need to do the right thing and sometimes that requires you not being alongside everyone else on the frontline. You have to be able to stand back and see the whole battlefield so that you can make the tough strategic calls when they're needed.'

This crisis was obviously an extremely stressful experience for Niall, so what was it that made it seem inspirational to him? 'It wasn't the act of failure itself, but the fact I'd come *through* a failure, having learnt things about myself and life more generally that I hadn't known until then,' he explains. 'I certainly became more tolerant as a leader. I understood better that if people are going to take on challenging roles, there will be times when they might fail. My job as a leader is to help pick them up as best I can when it happens.'

Warren Bennis, the acclaimed business academic and author, has termed experiences of the kind Niall FitzGerald went through during the Persil Power crisis as the *crucibles* of leadership. The term is linked intriguingly to our analogy of leadership inspiration being a process of alchemy, as crucibles were the vessels originally used by medieval alchemists in their attempts to turn base metals into gold.

Bennis found that when leaders are tested by difficult and sometimes harrowing circumstances, they are forced to question their personal assumptions, values and capabilities. As a result, these experiences are often transformational for them. People tend to emerge stronger and wiser, with an altered sense of their personal identity and of their role as leaders.

Discovering inspiration as a leader is certainly not always a comfortable process, but at least we can be confident that this form of alchemy has the genuine potential to deliver the transformative results it promises. As the leaders we have heard from so far have demonstrated, when the right confluence occurs between our motivations, mindsets and experiences, a magical surge in our spirits and motivation becomes not only possible, but actually quite likely.

So how does this inspiration manifest itself in practice? What does inspiration actually look and feel like? And how can we ensure we enjoy the fruits of inspiration in all its potential guises? It is to these questions we will now turn as we progress to explore how leaders describe their personal *experience* of inspiration.

EXTERNAL TRIGGERS: IN SUMMARY...

- As our lives unfold over time, there are a plethora of influences that gradually, layer by layer, shape who we become as individuals.

- As we look back over time, there is usually a small handful of outstanding events, situations or people we can identify that have played a defining role in our development as leaders.

- The triggers that inspire us are not inherently inspirational in their own right – their influence is dependent upon the mindset we bring to interpret them and the way they relate to our deepest motivations and values.

- Of all the potential triggers for leadership inspiration, people such as our parents, bosses, customers, staff and colleagues seem to be some of the most significant.

- Major events or milestones can provoke us to think in new ways and awaken within us a new perspective on ourselves and what we want to make of our lives.

- The circumstances in which we live and work over longer periods of time can have a major impact on our spirits, depending on their resonance with our intrinsic motivations.

- We don't have to wait in the hope that we might occasionally encounter inspirational triggers – we can choose to seek them out actively, so that we experience them more frequently.

- The experience of challenging situations or roles can be an invigorating source of leadership inspiration as they provide opportunities to stretch our personal talents to the limit.

REFLECTIONS 4: MY TRIGGERS

As you look back over your life, who are the people you have found most inspiring? What kind of impact did they have on you?

Who? *What impact?*

Which particular events or experiences have acted as important triggers for your inspiration as a leader?

What has been the biggest leadership challenge you have faced in your life so far?

What did you learn about yourself, your leadership and life more generally from passing through this challenging experience?

As you reflect on the various triggers you have listed here, what conclusions can you draw about the kind of things that most inspire you?

What three things could you do to increase your chances of experiencing inspirational triggers more frequently in the future?

1.

2.

3.

PART TWO

HOW LEADERS CAN *EXPERIENCE* INSPIRATION

DISCOVER		EXPERIENCE	MAINTAIN
	5	The Inspiration Timeline	
	6	Future Purpose	
	7	Present Enjoyment	
	8	Past Achievement	
	9	Illumination Beyond Time	

THE GOOD USE OF TIME
MAKES TIME EVEN MORE PRECIOUS

JEAN-JACQUES ROUSSEAU

5

EXPERIENCE	
5	The Inspiration Timeline
6	Future Purpose
7	Present Enjoyment
8	Past Achievement
9	Illumination Beyond Time

Isn't it extraordinary that your whole life has led you to this precise moment? You were born, you were brought up, you have done all manner of amazing things, and everything so far has brought you here. Reading these words, on this page. *Now.*

Just as incredibly, the rest of your life lies ahead of you – whatever today still has in store for you, hopefully a good night's sleep tonight, the promise of tomorrow, and the day after, and all the days, months and years after that.

Your whole life pivots on this one moment, just as it pivots on every present moment.

Our experience of life is governed by this inescapable progression through time. Even the moment you considered the word *now* in the first paragraph above has already slipped a few seconds into your past.

As time ticks by, we can look back on the past by reflecting on all our memories of what has happened and what we have been through. We can also look forward to the future, with all our hopes and fears about what may still be to come. But we only ever experience life itself and all these thoughts and musings in the moment we exist, in the present.

Just as our experience of *life* is determined by our place in this timeline, the same is true of our experience of *inspiration*.

As we discovered in Part 1, we feel inspired as leaders when we do work that plays to our *passions*, when we face challenges that stretch our *talents* and when we are using our lives to champion our core *values*. However, there are a number of different ways we can actually *experience* the resulting feelings, depending on the perspective we are bringing to our place in time.

As we look forward to the *future*, we can feel excited by a sense of possibility and purpose, a drive to achieve certain goals and to make the most of the time we have remaining.

As we experience the *present*, we can feel exhilarated by our enjoyment of the work we are involved in, the people we are connected with and the influence we are having on the world around us.

As we look back on the *past,* we can feel boosted by our achievements, giving us a sense of fulfilment and a growing belief in our own capability and potential.

Finally, just occasionally, our awareness can lift *beyond time*, when our perspective rises above the confines of our current situation. It is at moments like this when we can gain an enriching sense of illumination about who we really are as individuals, what matters to us most in life and how we can make a bigger difference through the lives we lead.

Taken together, all of these forms of inspiration are manifestations of our core desire to make the most of ourselves and to fulfil our potential to have a positive impact in the world. They differ simply in how they relate to our experience of life's ongoing timeline.

We will explore the way time influences our experience of inspiration in more detail in this chapter. We will then move on, in the remaining chapters of Part 2, to investigate each of the four different types of leadership inspiration in turn.

A policeman's lot

Gary Hilton had been keeping his eye nervously on his phone all day. Having recently been through a promotion process for the role of superintendent in Merseyside Police, he was waiting for a call from the chief constable to let him know the outcome.

We have all been there. When you are waiting to hear the results of something important like this, time can pass s-l-o-w-l-y!

In fact Gary *had* been there before. Eighteen months previously he had made a similar application and not been successful. So even more was riding on this decision for him than usual, especially since he had already been acting in the superintendent role for the past few months.

To understand the significance of this moment for Gary, it is important to know something of his personal background. He was brought up on a tough social housing estate in the North West of England in the 1960s and 1970s. He never knew his father and his step dad died when he was just ten years old.

During his early teenage years, Gary's mother began having a few new relationships. 'Being brought up by your mum in a single parent environment, it's inevitable that men will be invited into your world,' Gary reflects. 'When it happens, though, at a time when you're making the transition from boy to young man, it doesn't seem fair. I was sticking out my chest as a 13-year-old, full of testosterone, trying to carve out our way forward in life.'

These years proved to be a defining period for Gary. 'That's when I think my values were formed, in relation to my mum, my sister and my mates at school. If you cut me in half and you look at the circles that make me up, there are certain things I believe in – fairness, honesty, personal strength, looking after others, stretching yourself. It's really these things that have been the source of my drive and inspiration ever since.'

Gary's decision to go into the police was influenced heavily by these formative experiences. 'When I boil it down, the thing that helped drive me forward over the years was the fact I knew I was always trying to look after people, especially people in vulnerable situations,' he reveals.

Gary had come up through the ranks of the police, from constable to sergeant, and then on to inspector and chief inspector. The formal move into a superintendent's role would increase his responsibility substantially to cover a team of 550 people. 'The job involved ensuring the operational delivery of our service across all aspects of burglary, assault, dwelling, drugs, traffic, in-crime investigation – the whole shooting match,' he recalls.

An inspired leader in action

When the phone rang at last, Gary's heart sank when he saw that it was only the assistant chief constable calling. But that all changed when she told him she had the pleasure of congratulating him on his promotion to the role of superintendent in the borough of Liverpool South.

'My immediate reaction was actually relief – thank God for that!' Gary concedes. 'It was only a week or two later that the real elation and excitement kicked in. It was then I realized they had given me the authority to shape and change the way things work in this area called Liverpool South. I certainly felt a sense of personal achievement, but more importantly an appreciation, a sense that they trusted me and had confidence in me to get on and do the job.'

As Gary looks back now on his career as a policeman, it was in this role as superintendent that he felt most inspired as a leader. It was the time when he had attained the hierarchical position and influence necessary to make a real difference in a way he believed was important.

'People typically get in touch with the police at their most vulnerable moments,' he continues. 'I wanted every single one of us to look smart, to know what we're doing and to work in a style of sympathy and empathy to the victims – first time, every time. That was the challenge ahead, that was what inspired me.'

As he became more senior in the force, Gary's sense of purpose to protect and care for people evolved in an important way. 'My focus shifted more and more to looking after the police officers themselves, the people who were going to put themselves in harm's way. What inspired me? I think it was the sense of responsibility to make sure I was doing all I could to look after them when they had to go out to face that real, critical danger.'

The depth of this emotional commitment to his team manifested itself in other ways too. 'I felt it an absolute privilege to have been asked to lead these people. I saw my job as taking responsibility for what they do, using my leadership style and the behaviour of my senior team to create a picture for everyone, every day, of what was expected of them.'

Gary's perspective on leadership had been shaped by the people he had served under himself, earlier in his career. 'Some bosses were all over the place and they'd just leave you feeling confused,' he explains. 'The ones I admired most were clear and consistent, so you knew where you were with them. They would praise you if you'd done well, but they certainly weren't soft – they'd challenge you hard at times if you needed it.'

One of these aspirational role models had been Superintendent Ted Greenwell. 'He had a skill in knowing people's names and he was so authentic in the way he dealt with every one of them.' As an example of his personal touch, when Gary got promoted at an earlier point in his career, Ted rang him at home to give him the good news. But before informing him directly, he asked Gary to put his wife Susan on the phone so that he could tell her first and explain how proud she should be of him. 'People like Ted inspired me. I can remember sitting there and thinking that this is how I want *my* people to feel. It's a gift.'

The role of time in inspiration

The way in which Gary Hilton discovered inspiration in his role as a superintendent in Liverpool South was very much in line with the process of alchemy we explored in Part 1.

His inspiration was *triggered* by the promotion itself and his interactions with role models such as Ted Greenwell. He brought a positive *mindset*, characterized by a desire to learn from his experiences and to be generous towards the needs and welfare of others. As a result, he found himself in a position where he was in touch with his intrinsic *motivations*: following his passions, making the most of his talents and living out his core values.

But what did Gary's *experience* of inspiration actually feel like in practice? And what insights can we draw to help us experience similar types of inspiration ourselves?

As Gary helped demonstrate, feeling genuinely inspired as a leader can result in a fabulous array of positive emotions. Excitement, elation, achievement, challenge, purpose, authority, responsibility, trust, confidence, authenticity, empathy, care, appreciation, privilege, pride. These are just some of the words he uses to describe how he felt during his time as a superintendent.

However, the way Gary expresses these emotions is not random. In the accounts he and other leaders like him give of their experiences of inspiration, there seems to be a compelling pattern in which four different *types* of inspiration can be identified. Each is distinguished by the unique perspective it has in relation to *time*, as illustrated in the Inspiration Timeline in Figure 3 below.

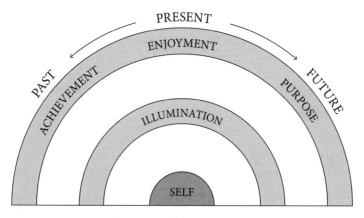

FIGURE 3 *The Inspiration Timeline.*

The future – A sense of purpose

One of the most fundamental forms of inspiration for any leader is an invigorating sense of *purpose*. The desire to make a tangible, positive difference in the world provides us with a powerful sense of direction and resolve as we look to the future. It also gives meaning to our lives more generally, helping to create a context within which our activities in the present and the past can be interpreted and understood.

Gary Hilton's leadership was fuelled by his desire to protect vulnerable people. He saw in his promotion to the role of superintendent an opportunity to put this mission into practice across the whole borough of Liverpool South. The scope of his purpose also expanded from focusing on the victims of crime, to incorporate the members of his own team too.

Gary felt excited, but also challenged by the increased level of responsibility he now shouldered. 'I wanted our performance to be extraordinary. I wanted our people to be extraordinary. So it was down to me to set the standard and make it happen.'

The present – A sense of enjoyment

The promise of what the future holds has a huge impact on our spirits, but so too does the reality of what we experience in the present. A second potential type of inspiration arises simply from the love of the work we do on a day-to-day basis. It might be our absorption in the challenges involved, the exhilaration we get from working with other people or the levels of influence and autonomy we enjoy in our roles.

In Gary's case, it was the personal connection and rapport he had with the members of his team that was most important to him. 'I used to walk in everyday and go round the office instead of straight to my desk. Seeing people, engaging with them, thanking them for what they were doing – that's what I loved,' Gary recounts.

'The police force is a very hierarchical organization and everyone uses the word boss all the time,' Gary observes. 'But the pride I felt most was when people called me boss and *looked me in the eye*. That's not so common, and it was the thing that made the difference for me.'

The past – A sense of achievement

As time advances, the things we do and accomplish begin to build up behind us in the past. The thrill of elation that accompanies important moments of success subsides over time to leave a more enduring sense of *achievement*. As the promise of our purpose begins to be fulfilled in practice, the result is a growing level of self-confidence, gratitude and legacy.

Gary Hilton's promotion is a good example of a personal achievement. He felt a degree of pride, accomplishment and self-validation at having ascended the ranks of the police to attain the role of superintendent. But any potential for him to feel complacent or arrogant was offset by the strong sense of appreciation, honour and responsibility that he also associated with his success.

For many leaders, the achievements of their *team* can be an especially important source of inspiration. As Gary reflects, 'What really inspired me was watching and being told about ordinary people in my team doing *extra*ordinary things.' He gives particular examples of young police officers bravely entering dangerous situations or attending shocking scenes of violent crime. 'I was so proud of what these people achieved. It's like being a parent. It made all the other, more difficult stuff that inevitably came with the job pale into insignificance.'

The legacy one leaves as a leader is not just defined by the things one has done or delivered. At least as significant for some is the impact they have had on the people they have worked with along the way. 'Is it important to me how people will remember me when I'm not around?' asks Gary. 'Well yes it is – *very* important. It matters that people think I cared for them, that they could trust me and that they feel I've had a positive input into their lives.'

Beyond time – A sense of illumination

The final form of inspiration is a little different from the others in that it is not tied so directly to our place in a timeline. In some ways it can be understood to transcend or go beyond the confines of time. This type of inspiration manifests itself as a sense of *illumination* or insight into who we really are as individuals and how we relate to other people and the world around us.

Gary experienced a moment of this type when Ted Greenwell asked to speak to his wife about his promotion. Ted's actions triggered an aspiration in Gary to have a similarly uplifting impact on the people he would lead in the future.

A different form of illumination occurred in Gary's life during his teenage years, when his mother started having new male relationships. This experience forced him to take stock of his role in the family and had a defining impact on many of his values in the years to come.

Illumination about ourselves and our place in the world can take place in an instant or, as in Gary's case, over an intense phase of time. The experience itself is not always a comfortable one and can sometimes feel quite disruptive. But the result is a shift in our self-awareness and our understanding, not just of who we are today, but also of who we can potentially become tomorrow.

The inspiration timeline

The four types of leadership inspiration revealed through Gary Hilton's experiences are captured in Figure 4. In the many

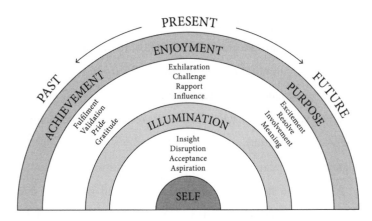

FIGURE 4 *The four types of leadership inspiration.*

conversations I have had with leaders in all walks of life, I have found these different forms of inspiration emerge from their stories again and again. Each brings with it a distinct bundle of powerful emotions that help fuel our spirit and motivation as leaders.

The benefit of distinguishing between the states in this way is that it helps us take stock of how we are experiencing inspiration ourselves today. Are we paying enough attention to all four potential states? Could there be opportunities for us to draw more inspiration from any particular perspective? We will reflect on these questions further in the coming chapters.

However, it is also important to highlight once again what the four states have *in common*. The reason they are all forms of leadership inspiration is that they all relate to our desire to make the most of ourselves as human beings, and to maximize our positive impact on the people and the world around us.

The emergence of a young leader

Sabrina Zurkuhlen is twenty-eight years old and has just been appointed head of athletics at The Calhoun School in New York City. Her experiences help to demonstrate how the Inspiration Timeline works for someone at a much earlier stage in their life's journey.

Sabrina attended Calhoun initially as a high school student, before moving on to study nursing at New York University. In order to help fund her studies, she returned to the school as a part-time volleyball coach for three years.

At the point when Sabrina had to do her senior thesis there was no school nurse at Calhoun, so she decided to design a proposal for a new school health programme. When she graduated, she started looking for jobs and was offered an exciting role helping to set up a new paediatric office through the Presbyterian Weill Cornell Medical Center in New York. However, in the meantime, Calhoun had decided to follow through on Sabrina's healthcare recommendations and offered her a newly created job combining nursing and teaching at the school.

The choice between these two options was a difficult one for Sabrina. 'The role at Cornell was awesome and paid probably twice what I'd get here at Calhoun,' she recalls. 'But it didn't have anything to do with teaching or coaching and I just realized that I wasn't ready to stop doing that. I was getting more and more interested in becoming a better volleyball coach. I was already doing a lot of professional development and building my knowledge of the technicalities. I knew I liked nursing, but I found I was *loving* the coaching, so that was why I chose this role.'

Since then, in a relatively short space of time, Sabrina's career has gone from strength to strength. After three years, she dropped the nursing part of her job to focus on the athletics coaching and she has now been promoted to head the department.

'My focus and passion has really shifted over the years I've been teaching,' explains Sabrina. 'Early on, the scoreboard success my teams enjoyed was important to me – it was motivating and gave me and the girls confidence. But now I've just gotten really interested in teaching coaches how to coach better. You've got to look at how people lead and help them figure out the values and philosophy behind what they're trying to do. That's the thing that really makes a difference, creating a culture amongst a team or a group of people.'

The Inspiration Timeline in action

Sabrina Zurkuhlen's experience provides another great example of the Inspiration Timeline playing out in practice. For her, the starting point was the sense of *enjoyment* she experienced when she was coaching her teams and seeing her pupils grow, both as athletes and as young people. Her early *achievements* built her confidence and encouraged her to expand her horizons.

As time has progressed she has shifted her role swiftly from student, to coach, to coach's coach. Her broader role at Calhoun is now providing her with an opportunity to put her new *purpose* into practice, by developing a team of coaches and creating a winning culture within the school. 'I live this, I breathe it – I believe in it so much,' she declares.

Sabrina has also become increasingly involved in Strive, a not-for-profit organization dedicated to spreading 'character-driven' leadership strategies among athletes and their coaches. She was recently appointed as director for their Summer Leadership Academy, a nine-day programme of activity run by a team of 40 staff for 125 coaches and athletes.

Have there been moments of *illumination* that have helped her find her way? 'I've had the pleasure of working with two incredible people – one here at Calhoun, the other at Strive. How they think, act and live has helped open my eyes and inspired me to think very differently about what I want to do with my life,' Sabrina reflects.

'There are also those everyday moments when one of your kids does something amazing and you think to yourself: "This is what we play for!" But I think generally my development has been a slow accumulation of knowledge and experience that has helped me to build a deeper appreciation of how we can teach most effectively. Ultimately it's that which has made the biggest difference for me.'

The Inspiration Timeline raises big questions for all of us, no matter where we have reached in our lives. What kind of purpose is driving us forward? Are we getting enough enjoyment from what we do every day? What kind of legacy are we building? And are we doing enough to seek new insights into what makes us tick and the potential role we can play in the world? We will explore each of these questions in more detail in the coming chapters.

THE INSPIRATION TIMELINE: IN SUMMARY...

- Just as our experience of *life* is determined by our place in time, the same is true of our experience of *inspiration*.
- Time provides the structure through which we understand how to develop ourselves, to build our capabilities and

- to increase our influence beyond ourselves as our lives progress.

- There are four different types of inspiration that leaders can experience, each distinguished by the unique perspective it has in relation to time.

  - A sense of *purpose* that gives meaning to our lives and fuels our drive into the *future.*

  - A sense of *enjoyment* that arises from the involvement and love we have for the work we do in the *present* moment.

  - A sense of *achievement* derived from our *past* success that builds our levels of confidence, pride and fulfilment.

  - A sense of *illumination* that goes *beyond* our place in time, helping us understand who we really are as individuals and how we relate to other people and the world around us.

- The reason all four are states of leadership inspiration is that they all relate to our desire to make the most of ourselves as human beings and to maximize our positive impact in the world.

- Distinguishing between the states helps us take stock of how we are experiencing inspiration ourselves today and where there might be opportunities to dial it up further as we move forward.

REFLECTIONS 5: MY INSPIRATION TIMELINE

Looking back again at your lifeline in Chapter 1, when have you felt most inspired as a leader?

During that time, how would you describe your sense of purpose?

What did you most enjoy about your role on a day-to-day basis?

What were your most significant achievements and how did they make you feel?

What were your most important personal insights or moments of illumination during that period?

As you reflect back on these experiences, be conscious of how you are feeling. Our brains work in such a way that when we recall being in a certain emotional state, we can sometimes begin to feel the same way again in the present moment. Are you experiencing that now? Have you felt your spirits lifting?

Choosing what we think about in this way is a very useful means of managing our energy levels. By guiding our reflection on our sense of purpose, our sources of enjoyment, our past achievements and our moments of illumination, the Inspiration Timeline can help us reconnect with these feelings of inspiration whenever we desire. We will return to explore how this can help us maintain our resilience as leaders in Chapter 10.

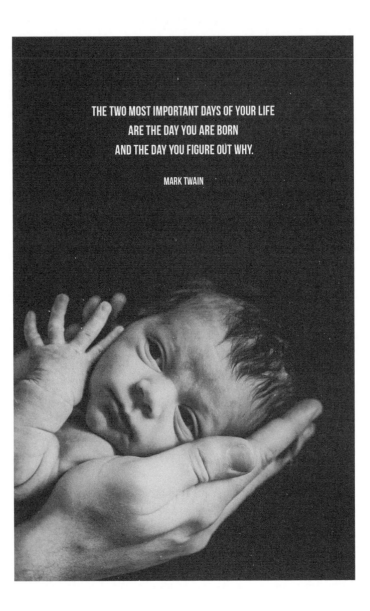

THE TWO MOST IMPORTANT DAYS OF YOUR LIFE
ARE THE DAY YOU ARE BORN
AND THE DAY YOU FIGURE OUT WHY.

MARK TWAIN

6

EXPERIENCE	
5	The Inspiration Timeline
6	Future Purpose
7	Present Enjoyment
8	Past Achievement
9	Illumination Beyond Time

Having a deep and heartfelt sense of purpose is one of the most fundamental forms of inspiration for any leader. If leadership is about changing the world for the better, our purpose helps define how we intend to go about doing so.

A powerful sense of purpose gives a point to our existence, providing us with something to live for and to work towards. It also drives us towards the future with a spirit of hope, resolve and a sense of self-worth and relevance.

We live at a time when there is a huge growth in people's search for purpose. As we covered in Chapter 2, the pursuit of materialistic riches is very often not enough to give us the meaning and direction we crave, especially with so many of us now living longer and wealthier lives.

As the influence of some religious institutions has declined, many people are looking to fill the resulting spiritual void in other ways. Commercial businesses in particular have responded by attempting to define the reasons for their existence beyond the mere creation of financial value for their shareholders. Their aim in addressing more noble causes has been to deepen their involvement with employees, customers and society more broadly.

However, with all the talk of purposes, missions and visions that has come about as a result, there is a risk we lose sight of what this really means for us as individuals. How does a sense of purpose actually manifest itself for people in leadership positions? And what kind of role does it play in fuelling personal inspiration?

Hearing the music

'Our mission is to fill every home with music,' proclaims Patrick Spence. Patrick is president of Sonos, a rapidly growing global company that supplies innovative sound systems to homes in over sixty countries. Its wireless speakers not only make it easy to listen to music streamed from the internet, but also to hear different songs in different zones of the house at the same time.

'This is a product I love – it changed the way my family and I listen to music and also the amount we listen to. I genuinely believe it will have a similar impact on people all over the world,' Patrick explains. 'An important reason for me joining Sonos was that belief in my heart that we offer people a great thing to make their lives at home better, and I'm very excited to play a part in bringing that to more people.'

Patrick is forthright about the importance of being clear why the company exists and what it is trying to do. 'We had a big kick-off meeting for the whole team last week and I closed it by going back to why we get up and come to work everyday,' he recounts. 'In addition to our mission, we talk about changing the way people listen to music in the digital age, one home at a time. It brings everyone together and inspires us all. Without something like this, I don't know how you'd do it. … I don't know *why* you'd do it.'

But Patrick's *personal* sense of purpose goes well beyond the passion he feels for the overall company purpose. 'There's definitely a sub-text for me around building a great company that's going to last for a long time. I also love the fact that we're going about doing it a bit differently,' he shares. 'We're still privately owned, we don't have a Silicon Valley presence, and we have some unique working practices. Lots of people say we're crazy, but I really like that – there's something about being different that really motivates me.'

The source of this motivation seems to lie in some important values and beliefs that Patrick holds dear. 'I think this is just the way I was born, but I truly believe that we, as people, are capable of so much more than we often think we are. I've played in sports teams when we shouldn't have won, but we did. I also spent many years working for RIM, and there's no way in the world a small Canadian company like that should have been able to build Blackberry into a \$20 billion smartphone business.'

'We did it by recognizing the only boundaries that exist are the ones you put on yourself,' he continues. 'I love the idea that by going outside your comfort zone and doing things a bit differently, you can take on the world and win. It's the sense of challenge involved that makes you feel so determined to succeed.'

Achieving the impossible

Does Patrick have some form of personal mission statement to guide him as a leader? 'I didn't before, but after the psychoanalysis involved in preparing for this discussion, I have now!' he admits. 'I think my purpose is to bring awesome people together and help them achieve something they never thought possible. When I've watched that happen – actually seen people do things they thought were impossible – for me it's the greatest thing on earth.'

When it comes to considering the role that a vision of the future plays in his sense of purpose, Patrick is more circumspect. 'In my opinion you have to be a little careful. I think it's useful to have a rough vision of where you want to be in the future, but you have to be a bit flexible with the details. Otherwise you might get locked into a path that ceases to be relevant when the circumstances change.'

He likens this to the way he thinks about his own career development. 'You never quite know what kind of opportunities are going to come up, so you can't plan your career in too much detail. I always had a sense I would end up leading something, but I never knew quite what,' he explains. 'We all have an ego and you have to take your own interests into account to some extent. But my view has always been that if I do what's right for the company today, our success in the future will open up doors for me personally as well.'

The spirit of purpose

When Patrick shares his sense of purpose, be brings a tremendous energy to the way he describes what he is up to. This is something

I have experienced frequently in my conversations with inspired leaders. As soon as they start talking about what they are leading *for*, their eyes light up and the passion flows. I would go as far as to say that it is one of the ways of *spotting* an inspired leader.

What kind of spirit is present when a burning sense of purpose catches fire within us?

Excitement about future possibilities

The starting point is to highlight the importance of an orientation towards the future. My great friend and mentor Steve Radcliffe is the author of the excellent book *Leadership: Plain and Simple*. In this he makes the point that leadership always starts with the ideas you have about what you would like to see in the future.

As leaders, we are drawn forward by a belief that in some way tomorrow can be better than today. We feel excited about the possibilities and opportunities ahead of us. Our hopes and dreams help us deal with the challenges of the present and propel us onwards with feelings of positivity and optimism.

In Patrick's case, this excitement manifests itself in a number of ways – in the role Sonos's products can play in changing the way people listen to music, in the kind of successful and unconventional company Sonos itself can become, and in the way the people in his team can personally develop and succeed.

Resolve to meet a challenge

There is a big difference between being excited by the promise of the future and actually fulfilling it in reality. Patrick's ambitions for the future are not just wishful thinking. The sense of challenge he feels in pulling off these feats has stimulated within him a deep resolve to make them happen in practice. He sees both an opportunity and a responsibility to make a special difference, by applying his own unique blend of experience, skills and personal qualities.

Patrick may describe his vision of what he wants to achieve as 'rough', in order that it provides some room for manoeuvre if conditions change. But that makes him no less determined to rise to the challenge and to make a big impact on the scope and performance of the Sonos business in the years ahead.

Personal involvement and commitment

Part of the reason Patrick's commitment is so strong is that he feels a deep sense of personal involvement in the Sonos enterprise and the role he plays within it. He has a passion for music and he loves the work involved in building and supporting the people in his team. He enjoys leading by example and derives particular satisfaction from coaching people individually, encouraging them to play to their strengths and go beyond their comfort zones.

As Patrick acknowledges, it is also important to recognize that a leader's commitment to a cause is rarely entirely altruistic. For a sense of purpose to be truly inspiring, it must be grounded in our *intrinsic* motivations. However, our personal involvement can only be enhanced if alignment also exists with our *extrinsic* motivations – our desire for respect, status, financial rewards and promotion to bigger and better roles. It is when we achieve *integration* between these various forms of motivation that our commitment levels will be at their highest.

A deep sense of meaning

Finally, and perhaps most significantly, a sense of purpose enables us to find meaning in our lives because it is fuelled by what we value and care about most deeply. Patrick talked about helping great people achieve things they never thought possible. This mission is made so inspiring for him by the fact that it is driven by some of his most fundamental beliefs – that we are all capable of more than we think we are and that it is possible to take on the conventions of the world and win.

The question 'why'

Together, these four ingredients help to explain what it *feels* like to have an inspiring spirit of purpose. However, it is also important to point out the different elements that make up the actual *content* of a leadership purpose.

As Patrick Spence illustrated, whether you are an individual, a team or a company like Sonos, your purpose typically consists of a statement of both the following:

- *Vision – what* you want to change or make happen in the future

- *Mission – why* you want to make these things happen

In his well-known TED talk and book called *Start With Why*, Simon Sinek highlighted how important the second of these questions is to us all as a source of meaning and motivation. Our mission helps explain why we exist and the kind of difference we want to make in the world. Indeed, this element plays such an important role within our leadership purpose that many people now tend to call their mission their personal purpose in its own right.

It was interesting that Patrick Spence admitted he had only become conscious of his personal leadership mission recently. Until that point he had been inspired more intuitively by his underlying values and beliefs.

I have talked to several leaders who are incredibly passionate but who have not yet pinpointed the reason why. In some cases this is simply because they have not given it much thought. In others, people do not see the point, confident that they are making an impact without seeing the need to articulate their personal mission in a precise and pithy way.

However, many leaders *do* have a clear statement of their leadership mission, and my conclusion is that it can play a very powerful role for us as individuals. In the previous chapter we learned of Gary Hilton's desire to look after people in vulnerable situations. Sabrina Zurkuhlen described her passion to help coaches become better coaches.

As these examples demonstrated, a simple leadership mission helps ground us as leaders, rooting us in the unique way in which we believe we can make a difference. It provides us with a role that is stretching enough to take us beyond our current levels of performance, and broad enough to open up new avenues for us to channel our energies over time.

Crucially, a leadership mission provides us with a personal narrative that strengthens the fundamental sense we have of ourselves, by defining the role we play and the value it brings. As such, its relevance extends beyond our drive into the future, because it also helps us interpret and give meaning to the work we do today and our activities in the past.

Like Patrick, many leaders find their mission in the role they play helping the people they lead to flourish and succeed. Others talk about strengthening the organizations they are responsible for so that they leave them in better shape than when they arrived.

What really matters is that we each discover a leadership mission that has unique resonance for us personally. This can best be achieved by rooting it in the drivers of our leadership inspiration.

We can find *meaning* by making sure our mission arises from our core *values*. We can find *resolve* by relating it to a challenge that stretches our distinctive *talents*. And we can find *involvement* by focusing it in an area that enables us to play to our personal *passions*.

It is when these three conditions are present together, as we look to the future, that the fourth and final ingredient of a spirit of purpose will be experienced – an energizing sense of *excitement*.

Bringing our purpose to bear

Once we get in touch with our core leadership mission as a leader, the next challenge is to find ways to bring our influence to bear as best we can on the world around us. For relatively junior people early in their career, their focus will probably be on the relationships they have with their immediate colleagues. As leaders become more senior, their impact can extend to their function or department, their organization as a whole, or even the world more broadly.

Sir Richard Branson, the founder of Virgin, has an interesting perspective on this progression. 'It has always been my objective to create businesses with well-defined purposes,' he explains. 'At the age of fifteen, I started Student magazine to campaign against the Vietnam War and mobilise opinions of a young generation concerned about the world. Almost fifty years later, our newest investment in OneWeb is looking to create the world's largest constellation of satellites to bring connectivity and communications to billions who don't have access to the web.'

'As Virgin has become more successful, we have been able to reach more people, and change more lives for the better. It's all about scope and scale,' he continues. 'I now spend most of my time working on causes I believe in for our non-profit foundation Virgin Unite. I feel very fortunate to be in a position to shine a light on some of the world's biggest and most pressing challenges.'

An evolving sense of purpose

The phrase Virgin now uses to encapsulate its overall company mission is *to change the game for good*. Kerris Bright has the responsibility for helping put this ambition into practice as the chief marketing officer for one of Sir Richard's biggest businesses – Virgin Media.

Kerris is an experienced commercial marketer who had led teams at top companies such as ICI, AkzoNobel and British

Airways before joining Virgin. 'I love the idea of being a force for change and a force for good,' Kerris avows.

'The way I articulate my *personal* mission today is to help businesses, brands and people thrive through insight and inspiration,' Kerris reveals. Her words are clearly chosen carefully. They reflect a perspective on her potential role as a leader that was shaped by two illuminating experiences she had a few years ago, towards the end of her time at AkzoNobel.

In the first instance, Kerris had led some innovative positioning work on the company's main Dulux paint brand. The aim had been to carve out an inspirational role in helping consumers bring more colour to their living environments and thereby to their lives more generally.

However, Kerris's main focus had been on driving people's engagement with the brand *externally*. She had not paid much attention to the potential appeal and impact of the strategy *internally* among AkzoNobel's employees, until challenged to do so by her chairman, Tex Gunning.

'It was a moment in my career when I realized just what an important role marketers can play in inspiring people throughout the business, based on the contribution they make to the lives of their customers,' Kerris recounts. 'My key lesson was that being a marketing leader is about being more than an excellent functional specialist. I felt inspired with a new duty to lift the spirit and engagement of the whole organisation.'

The second experience occurred as Kerris was leaving AkzoNobel after ten years. As a farewell present she was given a book full of personal notes from the people she had worked with. 'It was deeply moving because many of them wrote about how I had helped and inspired them in ways I'd not really been aware of,' Kerris remembers.

It is as a result of these insights that Kerris now frames her mission to focus on three key areas of impact – business, brands and people. So how has this influenced her approach in her most recent role as CMO at Virgin Media?

Helping Virgin Media thrive

'I've always really enjoyed being in big businesses where you can touch many people's lives,' Kerris reflects. 'Although we may not be *saving* lives here at Virgin Media, I do think the connection we provide to broadband and entertainment is fundamental to how people *live* their lives these days. And with this being the Virgin brand, we have a fantastic opportunity to change the game by making good things happen for customers with a bit of creative flair and personality.'

'It's an incredibly dynamic industry to be involved in,' she continues. 'That brings with it some challenges, but I'm very excited about having the opportunity to be at the forefront of shaping the UK's digital economy.'

'When I joined a year and a half ago, the lack of a clear sense of the role that our brand could play in the lives of consumers had meant there had been a real vacuum in the company,' Kerris recollects. 'It was a huge challenge, but I've been excited by the fact that I've got the experience to do something about it. We need to make sure Marketing is coming up with brand ideas that do a brilliant job in engaging our customers, but that also provide inspiration and direction to our people internally too.'

Kerris has started to bring a more customer-orientated dimension to Virgin Media's business strategy. 'Commercially our business is all about growth and adding a million new customers, but we now talk more insightfully about connecting people to the things they love, so they can do more and have more fun.'

'We want to become the most irresistible brand in entertainment,' Kerris declares. 'We want customers to be with us in spirit and to feel a part of everything we're doing. We've certainly got a long way to go before we deliver against this in practice, but it's massively motivational to think we have got the opportunity to make it happen.'

Kerris is also ambitious about the impact she has on the people within the company. 'I want people to feel that I've made a genuine difference to this business, both in terms of the things we've done together as a result of my leadership, and also in terms of how I've helped them grow as people,' Kerris explains. 'Leadership is not just about the things you're doing. I understand better now that it's also about how you're being, and it's that which has the greatest impact on how people feel.'

As Kerris expresses her sense of purpose, it is interesting to note how the same dimensions of spirit come across so strongly once again – her *excitement* about the future, her *resolve* to meet the challenges facing her, the personal *involvement* she feels in doing so and the sense of *meaning* she gets from being able to make a valuable difference.

This leads us to some important questions for you personally. How strongly do you feel these ingredients are present in your own current sense of purpose? How clear and inspired do you feel about the difference you want to make as a leader? Now is your chance to have a think about these issues by engaging with the next set of reflective questions.

FUTURE PURPOSE: IN SUMMARY...

- A sense of purpose provides us with something to live for and to work towards, driving us into the future with a spirit of hope, resolve and a sense of self-worth and relevance.

- The spirit that inflames a burning sense of leadership purpose comprises a number of important ingredients:

  ○ *Excitement* – arising from the possibilities we see in the future.

  ○ *Resolve* – arising from our desire to overcome the challenges involved in making things happen in practice.

  ○ *Involvement* – arising from our personal passion and interest in the job to be done.

  ○ *Meaning* – arising from the use of our life to make a difference in line with our core values.

- If our vision of the things we want to change in the future is *what* we are leading for, our leadership mission helps to explain *why* it is so important to us.

- A simple statement of our leadership mission helps ground us, providing a personal narrative that enables us to make greater sense of the work we do and the value it brings.

- Our mission will have most resonance for us personally when it is rooted in the drivers of our leadership inspiration: our values, passions and talents.

- As we look to the future, our challenge as leaders is to find ways of bringing our mission to bear to the fullest possible extent on the world around us.

REFLECTIONS 6: MY PURPOSE

*When you think about what you are leading for today, what are the possibilities in the future that most **excite** you?*

*What are the challenges you feel **resolved** to address in the next 1–3 years?*

*What is it that makes this leadership agenda most **involving** for you personally?*

*In what ways do you derive a sense of **meaning** and significance from your leadership goals?*

Taking into account the Passions, Talents and Values you identified in Chapter 2, try to capture your personal purpose in the form of two simple Leadership Vision and Mission statements.

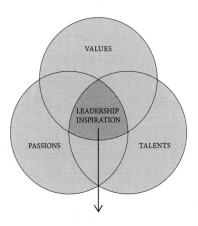

Leadership Vision

What do you want to change or make happen in the future?

Leadership Mission

Why do you want to make these things happen?
(or to put it another way, what is the difference you want to make?)

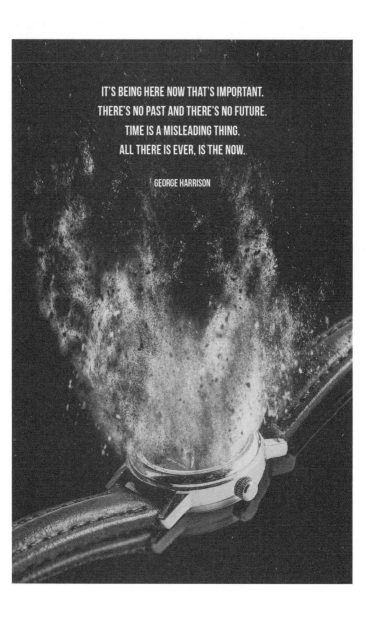

IT'S BEING HERE NOW THAT'S IMPORTANT.
THERE'S NO PAST AND THERE'S NO FUTURE.
TIME IS A MISLEADING THING.
ALL THERE IS EVER, IS THE NOW.

GEORGE HARRISON

7

EXPERIENCE	
5	The Inspiration Timeline
6	Future Purpose
7	Present Enjoyment
8	Past Achievement
9	Illumination Beyond Time

Declan Donnellan is an internationally renowned theatre director who recently received the Golden Lion for Lifetime Achievement from the prestigious La Biennale di Venezia. The organization's board of directors acknowledged him for 'his capacity to bring the classical texts to a contemporary audience' and 'for having placed the actors at the centre of his work and brought out the best in them'.

Over the years, Declan has directed plays in over 400 cities around the world. He has served as the associate director of the Royal

National Theatre in London. In addition to his latest recognition in Venice, his achievements have also included four Olivier awards. He was made a Chevalier de l'Ordre des Arts et des Lettres in 2004 for his work in France and he shared the Charlemagne award in 2009 with Craig Venter and Archbishop Desmond Tutu.

What makes all this success so fascinating is that Declan's life could have taken a very different course. After studying English and Law at Cambridge University, he was called to the Bar in 1978. He soon realized he had made a mistake and that the legal profession was not for him.

'I remember having coffee in Chancery Lane with some young colleagues, arguing about some scandal that was besetting the government. One of them shouted at me: "You are so impossible! You always take the contrary view, don't you?!" and I started to wonder if I was cut out for that world,' Declan recalls. The defining moment came shortly afterwards, however, when he shared his concerns with an older mentor. 'He was a very kind and wise man, but I'll never forget what he said to me when I explained how I felt: "Oh for God's sake Donnellen, pull yourself together. You're not getting any younger – you're nearly 22!"'

'It was such a wonderful thing – the sheer crassness of his advice. Bad advice is always useful as long as it is spectacularly bad! He was full of good intentions, but that was the moment when I knew I couldn't consign myself to the legal system and to people who think like that any longer.'

A life in theatre

Declan admits to having been a 'stage-struck actor' when he was a student and so he decided to follow his heart and switch his focus to the theatre. He wanted to find a way to work with his partner Nick Ormerod, so they set up their theatre company Cheek By Jowl in 1981 with the purpose of re-examining the great texts of world theatre in fresh ways.

'Our goal has always been to have an emotional relationship with the audience who participate with us in this act of theatre,' Declan explains. 'These connections will vary in all sorts of ways as the evening goes on, but we've always come back to the need to have this immediate, vivid, lively interconnection with our audience. I think there's an incredible thrill to be had in making emotional connections with people. The important thing is that our work is *alive*, and if it's alive it's going to be involving and challenging.'

As a director, the emotional connection he has with his actors is particularly vital. 'Our work can't be any better than the standard of the acting, so we're all dependent on the actor's capacity to act. And the actor's capacity to act is dependent on the actor's confidence. So I see my role as a director being to help release that confidence. You do that not by giving false praise – that's a disaster in my experience. You have to sincerely commit to them as people and then be truly present, attentive and authentic with them as they explore their roles.'

Declan's creative insight into what it means to feel fully alive in any given moment gives him a unique perspective on how inspiration can be experienced. 'I think the fatal mistake is to try and achieve the *state* of inspiration. People spend so much time and effort trying to achieve states, create states, run states! The important thing is to be attentive, to live in the present, and to put yourself in better and better contact with people and the outside world in general.'

'The people reading this book are probably going to be looking for more information about how to feel inspired,' he warns. 'My advice is to stop wanting more information, because our heads are too full already.'

'The important thing is to *empty* ourselves so that we have the capacity to start receiving things. If we know everything, we can't learn anything. If we can get better at receiving things, we'll be better able to connect with the outside world in its purest form. I believe it's ultimately through paying attention to those connections that inspiration comes.'

The value of mindfulness

There are many lessons from Declan Donnellan's story and his points of view, but two stand out for me. The first is the far-reaching value of choosing a path in life that enables us to do what we enjoy and have an aptitude for. The second is that by involving ourselves more fully in our experience of the present moment, we have the opportunity to feel more alive and connected to the world around us.

As we go about our busy daily lives, it is so easy to get caught up in the steady stream of tasks to complete, meetings to attend and deadlines and targets to be met. The stresses and strains build up and we soon lose sight of why we are doing what we are doing and whether we are really enjoying it.

Our minds also have a natural tendency to wander and we can spend far too much time reliving past difficulties and worrying about potential future problems. We then bring these negative perspectives and the fearful feelings they generate in us to our current activities, undermining our spirits and our performance as we do so.

In our exploration of the Inspiration Timeline, we have started to recognize the value of thinking more positively about our purpose in the future and our achievements in the past. But even these thoughts distract us from the potential inspiration to be had from focusing on our experience of the present.

The growth in the practice of mindfulness in recent years is helping to address this priority. In essence, mindfulness involves consciously choosing to pay attention to what is going on in the present moment in an open, non-judgemental way. It involves leaving behind our preconceptions and opening up to the world, seeing things for how they are, rather than how we might hope or fear them to be.

There are essentially two types of mindfulness practice. The first is more informal and is closely related to the approach championed by Declan Donnellan. This form involves being more present, attentive and aware of what we are thinking from moment to moment as we go about our everyday life.

The second approach is more formal in that it involves taking time out of the day to be still, reflective and to carry out various types of meditative practice. To provide an example of the benefits of this second approach, let us return to Sir Richard Branson, who recently published a compelling blog post on the subject. Here is an excerpt:

If you allow yourself to be in the moment, and appreciate the moment, happiness will follow. I speak from experience. We've built a business empire, joined conversations about the future of our planet, attended many memorable parties and met many unforgettable people. And while these things have brought me great joy, it's the moments that I stopped just to be, rather than do, that have given me true happiness. Why? Because allowing yourself just to be, puts things into perspective. Try it. Be still. Be present.

The experience of enjoyment

One of the most intriguing aspects of mindfulness is that it involves, on the one hand, a conscious lifting *out* of our experiences so that we can be more observant and objective about what is going on around us. At the same time, though, it means we can participate more fully *in* our experiences by being more focused and aware of all that is happening in any given moment.

This latter dimension of being deeply involved in what we are doing at any point in time can be a potent source of happiness and inspiration. To appreciate why, we need to understand the work of a pioneering Hungarian psychologist called Mihaly Csikszentmihalyi (pronounced Me-High Chick-Sent-Me-High if you ever need to say it out loud!)

Csikszentmihalyi set out to understand more about what it means for human beings to experience *enjoyment*, or what he describes as 'the exhilarating sensation of being fully alive'. His research has covered thousands of people from many walks of life, ranging from mountain climbers and dancers to pianists and chess players. His subjects were chosen on the basis of them being people who spend their time doing the things they most enjoy.

Csikszentmihalyi's conclusions have been consistent across a multitude of studies, irrespective of people's age, gender or nationality. He has found that whenever people feel a deep sense of happiness or enjoyment, they describe it in a very similar way. He has termed this experience as being 'in flow', because many liken it to being 'carried away by an outside force' or 'moving effortlessly with a current of energy'.

We all experience flow from time to time and you will no doubt recognize its key features. It involves us being totally focused and absorbed in an activity, to the extent that time flies by and nothing else seems to matter any more. Crucially, there needs to be a level of challenge where we feel a good balance between the difficulty of the task and our ability to handle it successfully. We must be clear about the goals involved and feedback is immediate, so that we get a strong sense of how we are getting on as the activity unfolds.

There is a close linkage between flow states and our intrinsic motivations because they are characterized by us being able to do things we inherently enjoy and that utilize our talents. Csikszentmihalyi also acknowledges the significance of integrating the different parts of our life over time and bringing a sense of harmony and resolve to our activities. He recognizes that this is achieved by discovering a higher purpose that is linked to our values and that gives a broader sense of meaning to our lives.

It is important to appreciate that being in flow may not always be a pleasant experience. Csikszentmihalyi's definition of enjoyment is linked more to feeling fully alive than to simply having a nice time. Our involvement and reward derive from the sense of being challenged and, as we learned from Niall FitzGerald earlier, that can certainly be uncomfortable at times.

It is also interesting that being in flow can move us away from some aspects of mindfulness, in that we can lose our self-consciousness as our absorption in an activity becomes complete.

However, the net result is an inspiring feeling of exhilaration and transcendence. A neuroscientific explanation for this is that when people experience flow states, they have been found to share the same high-voltage, slow-frequency patterns of brain wave activity as people engaged in spiritual practices or in blissful meditative states.

What leaders most enjoy

What are the activities that *leaders* find most enjoyable and exhilarating? How do they experience inspiration through the tasks they are involved in on a day-to-day basis?

Tom Willis, director of security at Heathrow Airport in London, realized early in his life that he was at his happiest when he was leading teams of people.

'When I was at university I studied Media and English and I remember us being split into groups to create a film. I soon worked out it wasn't the writing of the scripts or the shooting of the film that was interesting me, it was working with the team itself.'

'I gain a huge amount of energy from getting a team of people together and helping them achieve something exceptional,' Tom discloses. 'I believe the role of a leader is to instil confidence and belief. So the greatest moments are when you can create opportunities for people and then, with your support, you see them go on to do more than even they thought was possible.'

When he left university, Tom's first job was on the Operational Management Development Scheme at the Royal Mail. He was attracted by a job ad which promised new recruits the opportunity to lead a team of sixty people after just six months of training. By the age of thirty-five he had gone on to become operations director for South East England with responsibility for 15,000 employees.

Tom moved to join Heathrow in 2012 at a challenging time for the airport. 'We had just suffered a big blow to our operational reputation after heavy snowfalls had resulted in severe flight delays that winter. The London Olympics were also looming that summer so I really saw an opportunity to make a difference.'

Up to 130,000 passengers pass through the departure gates of Heathrow airport each day. Tom soon recognized the importance of his team's culture in creating the best possible experience for these customers. 'Our vision is to create a culture where inspired teams consistently deliver exceptional performance in safety, compliance, service and efficiency,' he explains. 'I'm very conscious of how influential I am in shaping this culture. As leaders, that's our role – we must create the right environment; we set the tone.'

His interactions with people are at the heart of Tom's own enjoyment of the job. 'I get tremendous inspiration from talking to our frontline people. That's where the action is and where we ultimately make the difference for passengers. If I'm having a bad day, I'll just wander into one of our terminals to have a conversation with a few people and I soon feel reinvigorated.'

Tom admits to having learned a lot about the value of consciously trying to see problems from other people's perspectives. 'Earlier in my career, I probably thought there was one map of the world – my map – and my map was the right map!'

'I now realize you create better maps of the world by trying to understand things from different standpoints. I love trying to put myself in other people's shoes. I challenge myself to have multiple experiences of the same discussion simultaneously! I certainly don't always get it right, but I'm convinced you make better decisions by having a richer set of perspectives.'

The leadership enjoyment dilemma

Most of the leaders I have spoken to talk of similar sources of enjoyment to Tom. Many describe the buzz and rapport that come from working closely with other people and being able to influence their mindsets and quality of thinking. Some leaders emphasize how much they value being involved in coaching conversations that serve to build people's confidence and capabilities.

There is also an appreciation of the responsibility that comes from being at the heart of what is going on in an organization. Leaders enjoy having the autonomy to make significant decisions that can change the course of future events and drive commercial performance and growth. In line with the concept of flow, many leaders also talk of their enthusiasm for the intellectual challenges involved in the strategic aspects of their jobs.

However, not everyone enjoys the same things and it is important to highlight a dilemma that frequently faces people as their careers progress. It is often said that what gets you to the top in an organization will not necessarily help you succeed when you get there. As we have started to establish, the mindsets, activities and behaviours involved in being a leader are different from those involved in succeeding at a more junior, operational level.

An alternative perspective on this principle, though, is that as you progress to become a leader, you have to *let go* of many of the operational things you have been doing – things you may well have enjoyed and been very good at. As a result, for some people, the step into a leadership position will not be one that suits them. Head teachers have to spend less time in the classroom. CFOs get less immersed in the detail of the numbers. Newspaper editors have to step back from the researching of their stories. It is by no means certain that these people's interest and capability for the new leadership aspects of their roles will fully offset their lost love and aptitude for the things they are leaving behind.

In business environments, there are two key leadership steps typically available to people. The first is to a position of *functional* leadership, where managers move to take on responsibility for a business department such as Sales, HR or R&D. The second is to a position of *general* leadership, where leaders assume broader responsibility for the business as a whole.

Choosing whether to advance in these ways is sometimes not easy, largely because it is difficult to know how well suited we will be to a different kind of job until we have had a chance to do it for a while. New assignments can often be uncomfortable as we find our feet, but the experience can be very rewarding once our capabilities and confidence grow.

The one liberating thought to bear in mind is that career decisions of this type are ours to make – and we *do* have choices. There are many paths open to us and it can sometimes be very beneficial to look for new ways to apply and build on what we have learned in our life so far.

Just as Declan Donnellan found, inspiration and success are more likely to be discovered by taking some chances and following our own heart's desires, than by pursuing the more conventional career paths that are sometimes expected of us by others.

PRESENT ENJOYMENT: IN SUMMARY...

- Inspiration comes from being present and attentive in the moment, opening ourselves up to connect deeply with people and the world around us.

- Mindfulness involves consciously leaving behind our preconceptions and seeing things for how they are, rather than how we might hope or fear them to be.

- We feel most alive and exhilarated when we get involved in challenging tasks that absorb our attention and stretch our capabilities.

- The activities leaders find most inspiring include working with the people in their teams and influencing the strategic direction of their organizations.

- Becoming a leader means giving up many of the operational activities that we enjoy and are good at – a change in focus that will not suit everyone.

- We have the freedom to choose a career path that enables us to do what we truly enjoy, rather than one that others think we should follow.

REFLECTIONS 7: MY ENJOYMENT

To start this exercise, take some time out for a minute or two to focus your mind on yourself and how you are being in this present moment. How are you sitting? How slowly and deeply are you breathing? Try and clear your mind and focus on your physical presence in the here-and-now for a short while.

How would you describe the way you are feeling right now?

Now let's shift mode a little. Have a flick through your diary – back in time and then forward, for a month or so in each case. Which are the activities you most enjoy and look forward to? What are the reasons they appeal to you?

Things I enjoy   *What are the reasons?*

Can you think of a moment at work recently when you were 'in flow' – totally involved in a leadership activity that you found absorbing, challenging and enjoyable? Describe what you were doing and how it made you feel.

What steps could you take to spend more of your time doing the things you most enjoy?

CELEBRATE WHAT YOU'VE ACCOMPLISHED,
BUT RAISE THE BAR A LITTLE HIGHER
EACH TIME YOU SUCCEED.

MIA HAMM

8

EXPERIENCE	
5	The Inspiration Timeline
6	Future Purpose
7	Present Enjoyment
8	Past Achievement
9	Illumination Beyond Time

Big projects completed successfully, awards won, targets hit, complicated contracts signed. In all of these situations, leaders feel a surge of elation and joy, followed in time by a more reflective sense of accomplishment and pride.

As events unfold, leaders can begin to see the promise of the purpose they have been striving towards delivered in practice. As evidence accumulates that they are really making a difference, they can start to experience a deep sense of fulfilment that they are leaving a lasting legacy.

It is only possible for any of us to access these feelings of achievement if we have been engaged in various forms of challenge. As we discovered in Chapter 2, human beings have a fundamental desire to build a sense of competence – to solve problems, to master complex tasks and to do things better or more efficiently than in the past. We are always looking for ways to test our capabilities, our effort and our character. Indeed, as we saw earlier with Patrick Spence's experience at Sonos, the bigger the challenge, the more intense the potential emotional rewards can be.

Challenges provide us with opportunities to prove ourselves, building our credibility and esteem in the eyes of others. We also seek people's appreciation for the things we have done and their gratitude for the efforts we have put in to doing them.

The motivation we feel is often at least as strong to prove ourselves to ourselves. Achievements help build our self-worth, confidence and belief. They demonstrate that we are developing and making the most of our talents, which in turn encourages us to embrace new and even bigger challenges in the future.

However, inherent in any challenge is also a risk that we do *not* handle it successfully. As a result, the fear of failure can sometimes be even more influential in driving us forward than any positive motivation. At times, the emotional payoff we enjoy from a success can be more a sense of relief that failure or defeat has been avoided than any more positive rewards. For some leaders, handling this balance between success and failure can be a fundamental challenge in its own right.

The challenging world of rugby

There can be few worlds where the challenges are physically more brutal than in the sport of rugby. And there can be few leaders in that world who have built up greater respect than Paul O'Connell, the iconic captain of Munster, Ireland and the British & Irish Lions.

Paul certainly had his fair share of success during a career that included two Heineken European Cup wins with Munster, 108 international caps and a Grand Slam with Ireland, and three tours with the Lions.

'I was lucky enough to win some trophies and the feeling at the time can obviously be very pleasing,' Paul acknowledges. 'The joy and ecstasy at the moment of victory can be quite overwhelming. You then have two or three of the best days of your life when you're celebrating together with all your family, friends and the guys you play with.'

Surprisingly though, these are not the achievements that Paul feels most proud of as he reflects back on his career. 'The winning feeling soon passes and you're soon worrying about the next match and your level of fitness,' he explains.

'I think achievement is probably one of the things that caused me the most problems in my career,' Paul reveals. 'I used to feel the whole season hinged on winning things. You either finished with a trophy or you didn't, and so you were either a success or a failure.'

The pressure that came with this perspective had a big impact on Paul's enjoyment of the game. 'To be honest with you, there were Friday evenings before the big matches where I'd have been very happy to get on a plane and leave the country,' he recalls. 'I would be sharp and snappy, arguing with my wife, my family and my dad. I'd look out of the bus on the way to the ground and wish I could get off and just be another person in the crowd.'

This pressure increased significantly when Paul took on the mantle of captaincy. 'I was always someone who spoke more than most in the teams I've been in. I actually spoke more than most of the captains I played for! So when I became a captain, there wasn't a lot of difference for me in the role I played with the team. The big change was the stress that came with the status and responsibility.'

'I'd grown up on stories of the legendary captains that had turned poor teams into great teams,' Paul continues. 'So any time we lost I took it incredibly personally, that I hadn't done enough to prepare or motivate the team properly.'

At the heart of his personal challenge was a battle during his career to overcome a series of nasty injuries. 'When you're the leader of a team, you have to be full of confidence and I got my confidence from my fitness. So I found it a real struggle to lead the team when I was only 90% or 70% fit.'

It was only later in his career that Paul found a way to deal with this problem. 'All you can do is your best. If you're at 70%, play to 100% of that 70%. If you've trained as hard as you can and prepared as hard as you can, you get to the stage on a Friday evening when you just have to say: "We've got to go and let the cards fall now."'

'I am certainly proud of the journey I've been on,' Paul reflects. 'Personally I feel my greatest achievements were coming back from major injuries and being able to take the field and play at my best even when I wasn't fully fit.'

'I only figured this out towards the end, but if it's only about success and winning, you'll never progress and get any better. To me the most important thing is knowing that you've done all you can to be at your best and to help other people be at their best too. All you can then do is try and figure out how to make your best even better!'

The role of a 'growth' mindset

To understand the transition that took place in Paul O'Connell's relationship with achievement, we must return to our focus in

Chapter 3 and examine further the role that mindsets can play in influencing our spirit and motivation. Carol Dweck is an influential psychologist who discovered that people tend to view the challenges they face in one of two different ways, based on the assumptions they make about themselves.

If we believe the personal capabilities and qualities we are born with are carved in stone, there is not much we can do about them. With this kind of *fixed mindset*, any test becomes a fundamental assessment of who we are as people. If we fail, it is proof we are not up to it. Even when we succeed, there is a continual need to try and justify ourselves again, to look smart or to show we can win.

The alternative point of view is that our basic capabilities and qualities are assets we can cultivate. With this *growth mindset*, our true potential as people is unknown and it can be influenced by the effort we put in to developing ourselves and our performance over time.

The meaning we choose to assign to challenging situations can therefore have a big impact on our motivation and reward, and even on our performance itself. If we make success mean too much, we can undermine our enjoyment of the experience and also the positive attitude we need to perform at our best.

It is clear from the change in Paul O'Connell's mindset over time that he became more aware of these different ways of looking at things. There is more to be taken from both success and failure if our focus is on developing our capabilities, rather than testing them.

As Paul showed, we can also draw greater satisfaction from the effort we put in to address the challenges we face. We can view our performance more realistically in the context of factors that may be beyond our control, such as, in his case, the situation regarding injuries or the quality of the opposition.

By looking for lessons in everything we do, whether we win or lose, we are more likely to find ways to improve our performance in the future. And the ultimate pay-off lies in knowing you have made the most of yourself and your abilities, a sense of achievement that counts for more, in the end, than winning any number of cups or medals.

From 'me' to 'we'

Another important lesson for leaders from Paul O'Connell's experience is that achievement is not just about one's own performance, but the performance of the whole team you are responsible for.

The rewards that result from this more social dimension can be extremely powerful. Leaders value tremendously the camaraderie, rapport and community spirit that can come from going through a challenging time successfully together as a team. They also feel great satisfaction when their people achieve things in their own right, particularly if they have had a hand in opening up the opportunities for them in the first place and in providing coaching support along the way.

However, as Paul explained, the step up to lead can be a tough one too. One's own drive to achieve can be difficult enough to manage in itself. When the responsibility extends to cover the performance of a broader team, for some people the reduced control over the end results can be a significant stress.

Josh Boutwood is a young leader who has already learned a lot about the need to balance a drive for personal achievement with a broader consideration for others. Josh is twenty-nine years old and has established himself as one of the top chefs in the Philippines. In his role as corporate executive chef for the fast-growing Bistro Group, he is responsible for 1,250 chefs working across over sixty restaurants.

'I must admit that in the job I have now I miss experiencing first-hand the gratitude that customers feel when you've just cooked them a lovely meal,' Josh reflects. His elevation to a more senior managerial role means that his focus is now more on the overall company system than on the creation of specific dishes. 'In a way I'm now cooking for the thousands of people we serve on a daily basis,' he continues. 'Although I'm not directly involved in each of those experiences, I find a different kind of reward in the fact we're doing something pretty fantastic everyday on such a large scale.'

Josh has been very successful in winning culinary awards, something that he sees as being a more personal form of achievement. He has won a host of gold, silver and bronze medals in the Philippines Culinary Cup every year since 2012, including Best Chef in both 2013 and 2014. More recently, at the prestigious Food & Hotel Asia show in 2016, he was part of the winning Philippines team and carried off personal gold and bronze medals in the 'main' and 'appetizer' dish categories.

'Winning the right medals is very important as a marketing tool,' Josh observes. 'Newspapers and magazines really pick up on these things and so the competitions have played a big role in propelling my career.'

However, he acknowledges his attitude has changed since his first competitive successes. 'When I was younger, I wanted to show people what I could do. The awards fuelled my confidence, but if I'm honest, my arrogance too. Looking back on it now, the achievements felt a bit hollow and I think they had an adverse effect on me.'

'I became very selfish and too focused on my work. It wasn't until my partner and my small daughter turned their backs on me and left me for a while that I came to my senses,' Josh reveals. 'I spent a few months contemplating what I was doing. Do I really want to try and be the best in the world? Or should I just try and be me and do what works for me and my family?

I decided to take care of what's most important, which meant finding goals that were acceptable to both me and my girls.'

'I've learned to become more humble,' Josh goes on. 'In a competing scenario, I understand now that we're all equals trying to do our best. The achievements I've had recently, whether it be a championship title or a gold medal, they have been more fulfilling. I actually get a warmth from it where I can finally feel like: "Yes, I have really worked for that, I've practiced for it and I've achieved it." I hang the medals on my wall and they act as a reminder to me of who I shouldn't be, in terms of my arrogance and pride.'

The value of gratitude

Achievement is a complex motivation to manage. There are sayings we are all familiar with that warn of the dangers of 'resting on our laurels' and 'pride coming before a fall'.

Yet, at the same time, it is clear that achieving success plays an essential role in building the confidence we have in ourselves and the credibility we have in the eyes of others. Our motivation to go on and achieve bigger and better things is fuelled by seeing signs of success along the way.

The fact that we often miss the opportunity to draw what we can from our achievements is illustrated by the frequent calls in organizations to pay more attention to celebrating success and highlighting quick wins.

How can leaders best balance their desire for a sense of achievement with the need to avoid vanity, arrogance and hubris?

One beneficial way to approach achievement is by learning to feel *grateful* for success. No matter what we manage to accomplish, we cannot hold ourselves wholly responsible, just as in situations when we might fail. Appreciating the roles played by others and the objective circumstances supporting our performance can help us see things from a less egocentric perspective.

As we learned in Chapter 3, neuroscientific research is beginning to show that feelings of gratitude can themselves have a positive impact in boosting our sense of well-being and reducing our stress levels. Not only that, but there seems to be a virtuous circle at play within our brains. The evidence suggests that the more practice we give our brains at feeling and expressing gratitude, the more likely our brains are to adapt to this mindset in future.

To take things one step further, another virtuous circle can exist externally in the dynamics between our own feelings and those of other people. The more a leader expresses gratitude to others for their part in an achievement, the more those people will feel recognized and appreciated in their own right. Gratitude, therefore, seems to have an important role to play in fuelling inspiration, both for leaders personally and in their relationships with others.

A focus on the future

Another way to channel achievement so that it becomes a positive source of inspiration is to focus on viewing past success as a platform for future progress, rather than an end in itself. The experience of Lisa Anson, the president of AstraZeneca's business in the UK, provides a great example of how this can happen in reality.

A couple of years ago, Lisa and her team faced a seemingly intractable problem. The UK government was in the process of announcing a major childhood flu vaccination programme for which one of AstraZeneca's products would be a key component. However, just at the critical moment, the company faced an unexpected and highly disruptive stock availability problem.

This challenge struck at the very heart of the way Lisa Anson views her purpose as a leader. 'I'm very motivated by making a difference and the more senior I have got here at AstraZeneca, the more I realize that giving people access to the medicines they need is something really worth fighting for.'

Here was a situation where Lisa's purpose was being put to the test. 'I knew that how I reacted was going to have a big impact on whether we would solve the problem or not,' she recollects. 'Underneath I knew I could never guarantee we'd be able to deliver what was needed, but my attitude with the team was: "We are *going* to do this, we are *going* to find a way."'

Sure enough, potential sources of stock were eventually identified in the United States and the necessary licences were granted by the regulators in an unprecedentedly short amount of time. The vaccination programme went ahead as planned, benefitting over a million children in the process.

'We moved mountains to make it happen and we managed to avert a complete disaster,' Lisa explains. 'People worked all night and all weekend. We were on the phone every hour to the government, the regulators and our US colleagues. In the end, the chief medical officer said that the way AstraZeneca had handled the crisis was unbelievable.'

The key lesson in this story lies not in the achievement itself, but in how Lisa has leveraged it since. 'It made me realize just how important our attitude is in making things happen. If we can combine ambition with a genuine belief that things are achievable, virtually anything is possible.'

Off the back of this learning, Lisa has launched a programme within AstraZeneca called The Art of the Possible. Each quarter, the management team comes together to share stories of success. 'The idea is not about trying to say that the impossible is possible,' Lisa clarifies. 'We're just highlighting exceptional performance from within the team in ways which inspire everyone to think differently about their limits.'

Just as in the case of gratitude, there is an interesting virtuous circle of inspiration at play in these dynamics. As Lisa Anson tries to inspire her team to greater heights, her own inspiration as a leader is fuelled when she sees it happen in practice. 'It's very powerful when you begin to see people thriving and doing great things. It comes full circle in a way, because I reckon I probably get as much of a kick out of it as they do.'

PAST ACHIEVEMENT: IN SUMMARY...

- A sense of achievement involves the experience of many uplifting emotions, such as elation, joy, pride and fulfilment.

- Achieving things helps build the belief and confidence we have in ourselves and the credibility and appreciation we have in the eyes of others.

- Achievements help demonstrate that we are developing and making the most of our talents, which in turn encourages us to embrace new and even bigger challenges in the future.

- Achievement can only be experienced by engaging in a challenge, which means the risk of failure is always present.

- The way we make meaning of success and failure is influenced by whether we bring a *fixed* or a *growth* mindset.

- It is the camaraderie, rapport and success of others that leaders value most when achieving things as a team.

- Leaders can avoid the pitfalls of arrogance and complacency by learning to feel grateful for their achievements and viewing them as platforms for further progress in the future.

REFLECTIONS 8: MY ACHIEVEMENTS

What have been the most important personal achievements in your life?

What have been your most important achievements as a leader?

How would you describe your feelings when you look back on these various accomplishments?

What lessons and implications do your past achievements have for you as you think about your future purpose and approach as a leader?

IF YOU DO NOT
CHANGE THE DIRECTION,
YOU MAY END UP
WHERE YOU'RE GOING.

LAO TZU

9

EXPERIENCE	
5	The Inspiration Timeline
6	Future Purpose
7	Present Enjoyment
8	Past Achievement
9	Illumination Beyond Time

In our exploration of the Inspiration Timeline so far, we have looked at three different ways in which we can experience leadership inspiration at any given point in time. We can look forward to what excites us in the future, look back on what has fulfilled us in the past or we can pay attention to our enjoyment of the present moment.

It is important to recognize, though, that our perspectives in each of these scenarios will always be constrained by the knowledge and experience we have accumulated up to this point in our lives. The assumptions and mindsets we have developed play a defining role in our interpretation of who we are and the kind of opportunities that are available to us.

The wonderful fact is that, just occasionally, it is possible for us to catch a glimpse of something that lifts our awareness to a new, more enlightened level.

The fourth and final type of leadership inspiration relates to this sense of *illumination*. It occurs when we experience some form of revelation or insight that helps us see the world and our place within it slightly differently from before. We deepen our understanding of what really matters to us in life. We see exciting new possibilities that strengthen our sense of purpose and give us a new spirit of hope and ambition for the future.

The ways we can experience this kind of illumination come in many shapes and sizes. Some might be small-scale everyday occurrences, such as those Sabrina Zurkuhlen described earlier when she enjoys the thrill of seeing her students begin to fulfil their potential on the volleyball court.

At the other end of the spectrum, for some people these moments can be transformational, shifting completely their perspective on who they are as individuals and the directions their lives are taking. One such person is James Brett, the founder of an organization called Plant for Peace and a man with a remarkable life story.

A difficult start in life

One hot afternoon in October 1999, James was travelling through Peshawar in Northern Pakistan when he stopped to buy a drink from an old man blending fruit on the street. As he began to drink the pomegranate juice he had chosen, he was seized by an overwhelming sense of opportunity.

'It was quite a mad feeling,' James recalls. 'I just sort of sensed that something powerful was happening. I remember turning to my friend and saying: "I'm going to make a drink out of this back home." I know it sounds a bit crazy, but the idea consumed me – I couldn't get it out of my head. I just saw a serious product opportunity and I became a bit of an entrepreneur for a while.'

James went on to launch a brand called Pomegreat, which by 2004 had become a multi-million pound business. But sadly this was also the year in which James suffered a serious mental breakdown. To understand why, it is necessary to know something of the dreadful experiences that he had gone through earlier in his life.

James had been born into a highly religious family in Swindon in the UK. His mother had fostered nineteen other vulnerable children when James and his three siblings were growing up. However, for a long period during his childhood, James was being cruelly sexually abused by his grandfather, a local Church Elder, who was head of the church James's family attended.

When James finally became old enough to realize the significance of what was happening and raised the alarm, the impact on his family was devastating. Despite all the efforts his mother had made to care for other under-privileged children, she was left with the feeling that she had not even been able to take care of her own children properly. Tragically, unable to come to terms with this fact, she committed suicide by jumping from the roof of a car park in Swindon.

The impact on James was also dramatic. For many years he grappled with drug addiction and depression, spending various stretches of time living rough and in prison. Several of his closest friends died from overdoses and one is still serving a life sentence in prison for murdering a drug dealer.

For a short while, the Pomegreat business had offered potential salvation for James, but he lost control of the company at the time of his breakdown and he soon had to start out on life once again from scratch.

From poppies to pomegranates

Events continued to unfold, however. During his development of Pomegreat, James had become aware of the importance of Afghanistan as a supplier of pomegranates. At one point he had talked in a news article about the opportunity for them as a crop to replace the widespread growing of opium poppies in that country.

In 2007, out of the blue, James was contacted by a lady named Dr. Julia Wright from a development agency called Mercy Corps. She had read the article and wanted him to speak on the subject at a conference in Afghanistan. As he was travelling through the Khyber Pass on his way to the meeting, James experienced his second inspirational moment of illumination. 'I just remember seeing fields and fields of poppies growing as far as the eye could see. It was a complete game-changer for me – I just knew I had to do something about it.'

This moment was more profound and emotional for James than the earlier entrepreneurial experience. 'My whole life flashed before me. I realized I had an opportunity to make sense of everything I had been through. I was a very angry person. I'm still a very angry person, but the difference now is I can see that anger doesn't have to be a negative emotion. If you have the gift of anger, you can channel it to make positive things happen.'

James set up the Plant for Peace Foundation shortly afterwards, with the aim of building a bridge between tribal communities in Afghanistan and multinational food producers in the West. He has started to enlist the support of companies like Holland & Barrett, Sainsbury's and Waitrose to provide new routes to market, not just for products containing pomegranates, but for other Afghan produce such as mulberries and walnuts too. His work has helped support a major refocusing of Afghanistan's agricultural strategy and significant progress is now being made in reducing the extent of poppy farming in the country.

James's own life has taken an exceptional turn as a result. He has addressed tribal gatherings in Afghanistan with as many as 14,000 farmers present. He has staged the ceremonial burning on television of heroin and opium with a street value in excess of $780 million. More recently, he has succeeded in engaging Prince Charles in Britain and the emir of Qatar to support his cause.

'I now see that everything I've been through has had a point. If I hadn't been sexually abused, I wouldn't have been able to handle the fear and insecurity that comes with working in rural Afghanistan. The injustice and hardship I felt after losing my mother is what drives me to correct the poverty and pain felt by the farmers. The loss of my friends to drugs makes me want to reduce the negative impact and conflict caused by the opium trade.'

James is now a man on a serious mission. 'This really could be massive – we've barely started yet. If I was running the 100 metres, my shoes would only just have left the starting blocks! There's no reason why the model we're developing couldn't be used by other countries too. There are 4 billion people in the world on less than $10 per day and these are the people we're talking about. I think this could be the biggest food cooperative in the world. I really do believe that.'

The impact of illumination

James Brett's experiences are extreme to say the least, but his insight into how it is possible to reinterpret and change the direction of our lives is certainly thought-provoking.

Moments of illumination are the purest example of the alchemy of inspiration we explored in Part 1. They are triggered by experiences that stimulate within us new perspectives on the world and the role we can play within it. Usually these come in the form of small boosts in our awareness, every now and again, gradually influencing our understanding of ourselves and the way our lives work. However, as in James's case, it is possible we might occasionally experience something more transformational – memorable moments that represent turning points in our lives.

At one level, all of these experiences can inspire us to *do* certain new things – to use our lives and our influence to make a bigger impact than we previously thought possible. Lisa Anson's launch of the Art of the Possible initiative is an example, prompted by her realization about the importance of a positive attitude in making things happen.

Illumination can also inspire us to *be* certain new things too. A potent catalyst for this tends to be our interactions with other people, particularly when they display values we believe are important. The moment Gary Hilton's boss, Ted Greenwell, spoke about his promotion to his wife was one such moment for him. We see traits in these role models that we respect and we then seek to emulate them in the way we behave ourselves.

What is so intriguing about illumination as a form of inspiration is that it can potentially be triggered by anything at any time – it just depends on how the people, stories, events and environments we encounter touch our deepest motivations. It is amazing how often serendipity comes into play, as in the chain of events started by James Brett's news article and the link it provided with Dr. Julia Wright and Mercy Corps.

We cannot choose what gives us a sense of illumination, but neither do we need to leave it to chance. As we saw in Part 1, there are certainly ways in which we can increase the likelihood of us enjoying the benefits of enlightenment a lot more often. For leaders, this is particularly important because illumination plays such a central role in our personal development and success over time.

The levels of leadership development

The way a leader acts and behaves is determined in large part by the manner in which they interpret their surroundings, and the level of awareness and sensitivity they have to interests beyond their own. As we saw earlier, when Kerris Bright was alerted to her potential impact on other people and on the cultural spirit within AkzoNobel as a whole, her understanding of her role as a leader went through two important shifts.

Developmental psychologists have identified a spectrum of leadership styles in organizations that are determined by the type of consciousness leaders bring to the many situations they face. Importantly, these styles also correlate with the performance of the organizations they lead, with the more sophisticated levels relating to superior commercial results.

At the bottom end of the spectrum are people who tend to be very egotistical, working in a manipulative and self-orientated manner. The developmental path then progresses to styles that focus more on the importance of relationships with others and technical expertise. At the higher end of the spectrum are people who begin to see things within their organizations from a more strategic and systemic perspective.

The most advanced level is when leaders understand their responsibility as extending beyond their organization, serving humanity more generally in ways that potentially bring about large-scale societal and spiritual changes. High-profile examples of leaders working at this higher level currently include Bill Gates of Microsoft, Paul Polman of Unilever and Sir Richard Branson of Virgin.

Illumination plays a crucial role in helping to raise the consciousness of leaders as they proceed along this developmental journey. Tom Willis's description of his change from relying on his own map of the world to seeking better understanding from other people's viewpoints is a good example. So is Josh Boutwood's reinterpretation of the role of his awards from fuelling his arrogance to reminding him of the need for humility.

The enlightenment involved is not only a source of inspiration for the leaders themselves, it also helps increase their effectiveness in driving the performance of the people and organizations they lead.

The role of the divine

Up to this point, we have explored the idea of illumination in purely humanistic terms, describing the inter-relationship between the potential triggers we might encounter in our external environment and our internal mindsets and motivations. We have not yet factored in the possibility of some form of divine inspiration, a vital consideration for anyone with religious beliefs.

Clearly this is a difficult question to address given the huge diversity of religious ideas and philosophies around the world. But let us spend a moment sharing in the experiences of one religious leader who has an unusually broad multi-faith perspective.

Inderjit Bhogal OBE is from a Sikh family who came to live in the UK from East Africa. In his twenties, he trained as a Methodist minister and went on to become president of the Methodist Conference in 2000. Over the years, Inderjit has been involved in many interfaith groups and led a national dialogue in the wake of the 2007 London bombings.

Inderjit has also been the chief executive of the Corrymeela Community, a group championing peace and reconciliation in Northern Ireland. Most recently, he has been the instigator behind City of Sanctuary, the movement committed to building a more welcoming culture of hospitality for refugees seeking sanctuary from war and persecution in the UK.

'I think one of the key challenges we face when we start exploring intangible concepts like God and inspiration is that we are limited by our language,' Inderjit begins. 'We have to use words which aren't really adequate to describe what we're talking about.'

'I have a deep sense that I am more than just me,' Inderjit continues. 'At a basic level, I can't do anything on my own. I need others around me – colleagues, community. But I also have a belief that there's a bigger, invisible reality – a strength I can rely on that is beyond me, but also within me. We have this short word for this experience called God. How else can I refer to this entity which is much bigger than anything I can possibly grasp?'

Inderjit refers to other leaders who have inspired him and who talk in similar terms. 'Martin Luther King had this moment in his life when he was threatened, with people attacking his house. He couldn't sleep, so he went downstairs and had a cup of tea. As he was sitting there in his kitchen, he had this sense that the God part of him was telling him that: "If you stand up for truth and justice, you'll find I'm there with you." And he went on from there to achieve what he did. So I read stories like that, and I can honestly say I've had moments like that myself. I have moments like that every day, actually.'

'Somebody who is not religious could say that this is just inspiration, and not necessarily from an external source,' Inderjit observes. 'But I believe there is an invisible reality. The difficulty is that as soon as I use language like God to describe it, it limits what I'm talking about because the word creates all sorts of pictures in our minds.'

Right place, right time

Inderjit had one particularly extreme religious experience back in 1986 that still provides a source of inspiration for him today. A young black man had just been killed in Wolverhampton as he was being arrested by the police. A massive demonstration was organized for the following weekend and the newspapers were predicting a war in the city centre. Against the advice of his church leaders, Inderjit went on the march wearing his minister's collar. 'I wanted to say: "The Church is here,"' Inderjit recalls.

As the protest developed, Inderjit found himself near the front line and he became conscious that there was no one providing any real leadership. He was soon at the centre of a flashpoint where the crowd was confronting the police. 'Because I was wearing the collar, people started asking me questions and I started answering them. I remember the media being everywhere, as they'd come to photograph the battle that was supposed to happen. I started shouting to the crowd: "If you throw one brick, you've lost the battle." "We want justice not violence." "Justice not violence." And very quickly everybody started chanting with me.'

Sure enough, the situation was eased and the march moved forward and finished peacefully. 'After everything calmed down, I was left standing there on the spot, shaking,' reflects Inderjit. 'I just thought, wow, what's just been achieved here? I felt aglow. I can't think of a better way of describing it. It was actually snowing, but I felt boiling hot.'

'I wasn't inspired to do that,' Inderjit explains. 'The inspiration came afterwards. It taught me the importance of following my gut instinct about the right things to do and the right places to be. I believe I was God's instrument in that moment. But you can only be God's instrument if you put yourself in the required place at the right time – it won't happen by you staying at home!'

Whatever we believe the sources of our own inspiration to be, there is no doubt that the enlightenment provided by moments of illumination can have an invigorating impact on us as individuals and our role as leaders. At times when we might be lacking energy or direction, seeking out new sources of insight about the possibilities open to us becomes an important priority.

In the final part of the book, we will look at this challenge in more detail. Having explored how it is possible for leaders to *discover* and *experience* inspiration, we will now conclude by focusing our attention on how they can *maintain* it – from moment to moment, over a whole lifetime and through the influence they can have on other people as leaders.

ILLUMINATION BEYOND TIME: IN SUMMARY...

- Our perspectives on who we are and the way the world works are constrained by our previous experiences and our resultant assumptions and mindsets.

- We experience inspiration in the form of a sense of illumination when we deepen our understanding of what really matters to us in life and exciting new possibilities are revealed.

- Moments of illumination can come on a spectrum that ranges from low-key, everyday experiences to transformational turning points in our lives.

- Our experience of people, stories, events and the situations we find ourselves in can all act as inspirational triggers of illumination when they touch our deepest motivations.

- Illumination can inspire us to increase our leadership impact through both the things we do and the way we behave.

- Leaders progress up a spectrum of leadership styles as their levels of consciousness become deeper and less self-orientated.

- People with religious faith believe that inspiration can come from a divine source, but our language limits our ability to comprehend such big and intangible ideas.

REFLECTIONS 9: MY ILLUMINATION

Have there been any significant turning points in your life?

What happened?   *What were the implications?*

Have there been any moments or phases in your life when your understanding of what it means to be a leader has changed? What did you learn?

Step back for a moment and have a think at a bigger level. Is there anything you are beginning to realize from reading and thinking about this book that you haven't quite captured yet?

PART THREE

HOW LEADERS CAN *MAINTAIN* INSPIRATION

DISCOVER		EXPERIENCE		MAINTAIN	
				10	Sources of Resilience
				11	Inspiration over a Lifetime
				12	Inspiring Others

DO NOT PRAY FOR AN EASY LIFE.
PRAY FOR THE STRENGTH
TO ENDURE A DIFFICULT ONE.

BRUCE LEE

10

MAINTAIN	
10	Sources of Resilience
11	Inspiration over a Lifetime
12	Inspiring Others

I recently had the pleasure of contributing towards a conference run for the leadership team of Siemens in the UK. In his opening address, Juergen Maier, the CEO, was surprisingly open about some of the challenges he has faced personally in recent years. The spirit of honesty and vulnerability he helped to create encouraged others to share how stressful they find some aspects of their life at work. In the most moving example, a young person bravely told the audience of over 100 people how they had battled to overcome a severe bout of depression.

Topics like these are usually kept under wraps in corporate life. We have to show up and play the game, covering up any signs of weakness or insecurity. Yet the pressure that many people are under these days is extreme, so it was impressive and very refreshing to see some of these concerns being addressed head on.

We discovered in Part 1 that the alchemy of inspiration occurs when our experiences, mindsets and motivations all come together to create a magical uplift in our spirits. In Part 2, we learned how we experience this inspiration in reality through our place in an Inspiration Timeline. In Part 3, we will now move on to explore how leaders can *maintain* their inspiration, particularly in the face of the intense pressures they are likely to face over time.

Unfortunately, the same process by which inspiration occurs can also work in exactly the opposite direction. When the circumstances we experience are more difficult and our mindsets less positive, the impact on our spirit can rapidly become very demoralizing. What are the difficulties and challenges that we find most dispiriting? And how can we find the resilience to rise above them and maintain the passion we feel for our activities as leaders?

Maintaining inspiration as a CEO

I first met Juergen Maier when he was in the middle of a typically hectic week. 'Sometimes I look at my schedule and it's unbelievable. This week I was up at 5am on Monday morning, off to Newcastle, back to Manchester, down to London, back to Manchester. Running from one meeting to the next. I tell you what, it's hard work!' He shakes his head and smiles ruefully. 'I know I'm not alone in this; many people have similar challenges. But my job is certainly intense and I do get tired at times.'

It is not just the physical demands of his role that Juergen has to contend with. 'I feel a deep sense of responsibility for the company and its people,' he explains. Juergen joined Siemens as a graduate trainee and worked his way up to reach the position of CEO two years ago. 'I started on this leadership journey then, but the journey the company is on is never finished. I've just got to make sure I do all I can to keep it going for the good of everyone involved.'

Siemens is the world's leading supplier of engineering and technology services. It operates in a variety of businesses ranging from oil, gas and wind power to road and rail transportation. The radical technological advances underway in its core fields of electrification, automation and digitalization mean that the company is under constant pressure to reinvent itself. Innovation is required not just to create new services and business models, but in some cases even brand new industries.

'If we get it right, there is a massive opportunity to create value and jobs, not just for Siemens but for the British economy too,'

Juergen observes. 'But get it wrong and we will lose out very quickly – it's an incredibly competitive and fast-changing market.'

Juergen's very practical approach to maintaining his energy levels in the face of these various pressures is based on the principle of *balance*. 'The way I work is to put myself into different modes,' he discloses. 'There are some moments when I just have to get into graft mode – clearing the inbox, spending a couple of hours getting stuff out of the way. I know I'm not drawing much energy from that, but I then make sure I balance it with other activities that I find more inspiring. A more exciting mode is being creative and strategic, when I'm thinking about the future of the company. Another one of my CEO modes is the inspire mode, when I'm on stage giving presentations or speeches; when I'm involved in external engagements or high-level meetings.'

Juergen's efforts to balance the way he spends his time at work extend to his activities away from the job. 'I do think there is a strong correlation between physical and mental fitness. If I'm honest, I don't do enough gym and exercise during the week at the moment. But one thing I do a lot with my partner at the weekend is to go walking or cycling, getting out into the hills around where I live.'

Which have been the times in his career that Juergen has found most stressful? 'As I look back, there have definitely been moments when I've not been sure I've got the right knowledge or talent required to succeed,' Juergen concedes. 'When you get offered a big new job, you can think: "Great, somebody has believed in me." But at the same time you can also think: "Wow, I've actually got to deliver this now!" That's when the self-doubt can kick in.'

It is at times like these that a leader's mindset becomes so important. 'I guess I have always had the optimism to say: "I'm just going to give this a go and prove to myself I can do it," he explains. 'I am the ultimate can-do person: "Let's find a way!"'

However, the most important source of Juergen's resilience seems to be his love of the job and his belief in the importance of the roles he and Siemens play. 'It's a tremendous job because I feel genuinely proud of the great things we do as a company,' he declares. 'We're delivering renewable energies, transport infrastructure, manufacturing productivity improvements. We see our purpose as literally helping to engineer the future of Britain. We're helping to transform Britain by making it a better place for its citizens to live in. We're creating more jobs and better jobs.'

'A job like my own takes a huge amount of personal energy and sacrifice, so you've got to love what you do. You've got to be convinced that what you're doing is the right thing and adding value,' Juergen reflects. 'I speak to lots of young people joining our company and I tell them that you need to make sure the job you choose really fits with your personal values, that you can live by it, enjoy it and be passionate about it. That's what makes it all worthwhile.'

The causes of stress

The potential sources of worry and stress described by Juergen Maier are similar to those faced by many people in leadership positions. Unrelenting time pressure, excessive workloads, intense competition and self-doubt are just some of the factors that can sap our energy as individuals.

Other demoralizing concerns people have shared with me include difficult relationships, frustration with organizational politics, disappointing commercial results, sensitivity to personal criticism and disappointment with the performance or commitment of other members of the team. There can also be personal issues to contend with like illness or relationship difficulties back at home within the family.

Whereas inspiration is triggered by a perceived promise of pleasurable rewards, stress occurs when we feel fearful and threatened. In physiological terms, an area of the brain called the amygdala senses danger and sends us into fight or flight mode. A distress signal is sent to the hypothalamus, the command centre for the body's nervous system. This in turn activates the adrenal glands to release the hormone adrenaline into the bloodstream, triggering a burst of energy around the body.

All of these physical changes happen in an instant, but if the brain continues to perceive a situation to be threatening, a second chain reaction is set off by the hypothalamus. This time a hormone called cortisol is released to keep the body on high alert.

The problems arise when our body's stress response system generates persistent surges of adrenaline and high ongoing levels of cortisol. Chronic stress can have a very damaging effect on our mental and physical health, with symptoms ranging from sleeplessness, digestive problems and weight gain through to high blood pressure, heart disease and depression. For anyone to flourish in a demanding leadership role, it therefore becomes essential to find ways to manage these risks.

The sources of resilience

Having spoken to a wide variety of leaders about the way they maintain their energy, it is clear that each of us has to find a blend of tactics that works best for us personally. However, a significant general conclusion emerging from my conversations is that the elements that contribute towards the alchemy of our inspiration – triggers, mindsets and motivations – are also the primary potential sources of our resilience.

Balancing our experience of triggers

In order to compensate for the stress caused by *negative* triggers, it is critical to seek out the triggers we know can help our spirits recover in *positive* ways. We need to replenish our energy by refocusing our attention and involving ourselves in experiences that we find both rewarding and renewing.

Tony Schwartz is a business author who has advocated a helpful way to think about maintaining this balance in practice. He has pointed to four different types of energy that we possess as human beings:

- *Physical energy* The energy of fitness and health that drives our ability to make things happen and get things done

- *Mental energy* The energy of thinking, reason and rationality that drives our curiosity, analysis and planning

- *Emotional energy* The energy of human connection and relationships that helps us feel valued, included, cared for and listened to

- *Spiritual energy* The energy of passion, meaning and optimism that comes from being connected to our core values and a future we believe in

One of the key principles involved in staying resilient is that we need to rejuvenate *all four* of these types of energy if we are to keep feeling fresh and fully charged. If our energy falls in any one area, the others will soon follow.

Juergen Maier emphasized the importance of maintaining his *physical* fitness by walking, cycling and going to the gym. Other physical energy considerations include getting enough hours of sleep, having a healthy diet and moderating our intake of alcohol.

Juergen's use of different work modes helps him manage his *mental* energy, by varying the types of intellectual activity he is involved in. Giving ourselves time and space to think and also maintaining our exposure to stimulating ideas and experiences are other avenues for mental renewal.

The crucial source of our *emotional* energy is our contact with other people. We must find time to be with our family, friends and the colleagues we find most positive and supportive. The more we invest in building generous and compassionate relationships with others, the more we will enjoy the benefits ourselves.

The fourth and final type of energy – *spiritual* – is the one most closely related to our experience of inspiration. We learned in Part 1 how this can be influenced by seeking out positive triggers, such as inspirational people and energizing challenges.

We also discovered in the exercise at the end of Chapter 5 how our self-reflection can help boost our spiritual energy levels. By using the Inspiration Timeline to guide us, we can focus our attention on reconnecting with the experience of the four different types of leadership inspiration. For example, by reliving past achievements or reminding ourselves of our leadership purpose, we can begin to benefit from the uplifting feelings associated with each of them in the present moment.

Maintaining our positive mindsets

Just as important as *what* we experience is *how* we interpret and make meaning of those experiences. As we saw in the cases of Claire Chiang and the Dalai Lama earlier, a shift in mindset can have a transformational impact on our ability to flourish in even the most harrowing circumstances. The first lesson from their stories was to face up to the reality of the challenging situations we might find ourselves in.

In some cases, the most difficult aspect of this process of acceptance will be not just coming to terms with the situation itself, but coming to terms with who we are ourselves. The reason we often find a particular challenge so stressful is that it is triggering negative beliefs we have about ourselves. Juergen Maier's fear over his ability to do some of the jobs he had earlier in his career is a good example.

By facing up to these limiting beliefs, understanding them better, and having the compassion to forgive and embrace ourselves for them, we have the potential to release the grip they have on us. In doing so, we can then begin to bring our best and most resourceful selves to address the issues we face.

Once we are released in this manner, the next step is to find ways to view the challenges themselves in more positive ways. If we can switch from a spirit of fear and threat to one of hope and opportunity, our resilience and creativity will improve significantly as a result.

Mindsets that can help lift us out of a negative interpretation of a situation include the following:

- Looking for opportunities rather than just seeing threats

- Reducing the significance of the issue by taking a longer-term view

- Putting the problem in context by taking into account the bigger picture

- Lightening the mood by seeing the funny side of the situation

- Seeing the challenge as an opportunity for us to learn, rather than representing an unnerving test of our personal capabilities and qualities

- Depersonalizing the situation by recognizing the problem is not just about us

- Giving our stress or suffering some meaning by relating it to a higher purpose.

Choosing to adopt perspectives of this type requires the calm mindfulness to take stock of what is happening in the heat of the moment and the responses it is triggering within us. The more we begin to practice thinking in these constructive ways, neuroscientific research indicates that our brains will adapt to use the neural pathways involved more often and more instinctively. Improved resilience will therefore begin to get hardwired into the way our brains work.

Aligning our core motivations

As we learned from Professor Deci back in Chapter 2, our general sense of vitality and well-being is dependent upon us meeting our basic psychological needs. As a result, the stresses we experience as leaders will seem much more bearable and worthwhile if the three intrinsic drivers of our motivation are being activated:

- *Relatedness:* We believe in the value to other people of what we are doing

- *Competence:* We possess an underlying self-confidence in our ability to handle the challenges we are facing

- *Autonomy:* We maintain a sense of choice and enjoyment concerning the main elements of the work we are involved in

As Juergen Maier argued, to establish the foundations for our resilience, it is therefore essential to align the kind of leadership roles we take on in the first place with our *values*, *talents* and *passions*. As the pressure mounts, it remains just as important to keep connected to these drivers of our leadership inspiration, so that we maintain the belief and motivation we need to see us through the challenges.

The broader the scope and responsibility of our leadership role, the more important these principles become. The higher we rise within an organization, the more is at stake and the further there is to fall if things go wrong.

In the eye of the storm

On 12 October 2006, Richard Dannatt, the recently appointed chief of the general staff of the British Army, unexpectedly found himself the focus for the evening's national television news. The *Daily Mail* had cunningly launched its Friday edition a little early to catch the 10pm bulletins. In doing so, it ambushed its rivals with the explosive headline, 'WE MUST QUIT IRAQ SAYS NEW HEAD OF THE ARMY.'

As the news analysis unfolded, General Dannatt had the unnerving experience of hearing recounted many of the things he had said to a reporter a couple of days previously, but given a very different interpretation. 'I did intend to speak out publicly about the issues I was concerned about, but I did *not* intend it to come across in the way it was presented, as a direct attack on the government,' he explains.

Having taken on the most senior position in the British Army a few weeks earlier, Richard's key concern was how stretched his troops had become, having to fight two wars at the same time. 'Because we were undermanned, and our manning level was actually going down, I felt the growing pressures of fighting in both Iraq and Afghanistan were probably going to have the effect of making our men go over a cliff edge.'

The apparent lack of understanding and responsiveness to his warnings at the Ministry of Defence had led to his initial decision to talk to the press. But his comments were seized upon as ammunition to use against Tony Blair's government and a political furore was the result.

A very upset secretary of state for Defence was soon on the phone expressing how unhappy he and the prime minister's office were about the situation. Richard accepted responsibility and committed to deal with the media proactively the following morning. 'The thing was, as I drove down to London and listened to all the radio stations through the night, the consensus was that what I'd said was right,' he recalls. 'I knew I'd touched a nerve in the country, so by the time I'd had a shower, put on a uniform and turned up for the live television and radio interviews, I was even more strident in my views.'

Handling the heat of the moment

For Richard to come out that morning and say the same things all over again caused consternation within the government and had a defining impact on his tenure as chief of the general staff. What did he learn from having to deal with such an intensely high-profile and exposed situation?

'The first thing is you just have to stay calm,' he advises. 'You've got to make yourself think about things and reflect on what is really going on here. What should my thought process be? How can I convert my thoughts into the written and spoken word so I communicate exactly what I want to?'

'You also have to believe you're right, otherwise you're constantly worried and looking over your shoulder,' Richard continues. 'It's when the doubts creep in that you start to hesitate. If you're in a combative, competitive situation, once people see you doubt or hesitate they'll go for you. They'll kick you as you go down, and kick you harder when you *are* down.'

That sounds fine in theory, but where does this belief come from and how can you be so sure you are right in the heat of the moment? 'Your confidence has got to be placed in the knowledge that comes from your experience and also from the rigorous, applied thought you've given to the issues and your decisions beforehand,' he explains.

Richard elaborates on this latter point by emphasizing the importance of decision making as an aspect of leadership, and drawing the distinction between two very different forms. 'In the field, you have to be able to make rapid, often instinctive decisions to deal with the immediate tactical situations you face,' he clarifies. 'But the more senior you get in staff roles, the more time you have to take decisions and the more far-reaching are their effects. That's best done by really making sure you've understood the problem, listened to other people's views and explored all the alternatives. It brings a critically important *intellectual* dimension to leadership.'

Richard is just as ardent in his view that one's self-belief and confidence is rooted in a *spiritual* dimension of leadership. 'The army has six core values that underpin everything we do in moral terms: selfless commitment, courage, discipline, loyalty, integrity and respect for others. These are very important – separately and together. But I think you also need something beyond this, something bigger. My Christian faith is an important part of that for me and has had a huge impact on who I have become, both as a person and as a soldier.'

Richard's commitment to these values and beliefs were the foundation for a deeply held sense of duty and purpose. 'At the highest level, I saw my role as being to serve the best interests of the country, the safety of its citizens and the well-being of the armed forces,' he declares. 'My main priority in this particular instance was not just to make sure the army would succeed on our behalf in Iraq and Afghanistan, but also to make sure it was set up to succeed in the next 10 years too.'

Taking time out

As Lord Dannatt reflects back now on his experience, he stresses the importance of managing stressful situations like the one we have just heard about by finding ways to keep a healthy sense of perspective. 'A demanding leadership position is, by definition, pretty lonely,' he confides. 'It's not a very British characteristic to unload to other people, but I think there's a lot to be said for having one or two objective and trusted friends or mentors you can talk to.'

'My wife, Pippa, was always good enough to listen and jokes that she's had to save me from myself on many occasions. But I think, if I'm honest, I would probably have handled some of the more controversial things I said and did differently if I'd had a habit of ringing someone up or going for a coffee and saying: "I'm thinking of doing this … what do you think?"'

'It's also important that you don't let the job you're doing become absolutely everything,' he continues. 'No matter what role you have, you need to maintain some other interests and activities that you can absorb yourself in.' Lord Dannatt enjoys fishing, plays a bit of golf and tennis and has maintained his involvement running the family farm.

'Apart from anything else, these other things give you some valuable thinking time,' he explains. 'I've always said the biggest enemies of an otherwise successful leader are an overfull diary and a hyperactive PA who fills a gap in that diary anytime one appears! Then you just become like a hamster on a wheel. The crucial thing is to generate a bit of space for yourself, to create an opportunity to get some perspective by putting some distance between you and your leadership.'

Once again, then, we return to the issue of time and the role it plays in influencing people's spirit and success as leaders. One of the senior business leaders I met recently made the following insightful observation: 'It's ironic, isn't it, that people like us spend so much of our time planning everything in our lives … except our lives!'

It is with this thought in mind that we will now move on to consider how we can find more inspiration as leaders, not just when times are tough, but over the course of a whole lifetime.

SOURCES OF RESILIENCE:
IN SUMMARY...

- The inter-relationship between our experiences, mindsets and motivations can have a negative impact on our energy levels, just as it is capable of having an inspiring one.

- The triggers that cause leaders most stress include unrelenting time pressure, excessive workloads, intense competition, self-doubt, difficult relationships, organizational politics, disappointing commercial results, personal criticism, being let down by team members and contending with personal and family issues.

- In order to compensate for the stress caused by *negative* triggers, it is critical to seek out the triggers we know can help our spirits recover in *positive* ways.

- Maintaining our resilience requires renewing four different types of energy: physical, mental, emotional and spiritual.

- A shift in mindset can have a transformational impact on our ability to flourish in even the most harrowing of circumstances.

- The most difficult aspect of accepting the harsh reality of a challenging situation is often not just coming to terms with the situation itself, but coming to terms with who we are ourselves.

- If we can switch from a spirit of fear and threat to one of hope and opportunity, our creativity and resilience will improve significantly as a result.

- To establish the foundations for our resilience, it is essential to align the kind of leadership roles we take on with our values, talents and passions.

- Giving ourselves time to think and to talk to others about our leadership can help us maintain a healthy perspective on the challenges we face.

REFLECTIONS 10: MY RESILIENCE

What are the things that most drain your energy as a leader?

What practices do you use currently to manage your four energies?
What could you do to renew them even more effectively in future?

Energy type	Current activities	New activities
Physical		

Energy type	Current activities	New activities
Mental		
Emotional		
Spiritual		

IT IS NOT THE YEARS IN YOUR LIFE THAT COUNT,
IT IS THE LIFE IN YOUR YEARS

ADLAI STEVENSON

11

MAINTAIN	
10	Sources of Resilience
11	Inspiration over a Lifetime
12	Inspiring Others

In 1888, a highly successful Swedish entrepreneur by the name of Alfred Nobel was astonished to read his own obituary. Nobel had built a business manufacturing military armaments and was most famous for his invention of dynamite. It was for this reason that the French newspaper responsible for the article castigated him, describing him as 'the merchant of death'.

Unfortunately the journalist involved had made one big mistake. It was actually Alfred Nobel's less well-known younger brother Ludwig who had died. Nevertheless, his article went on to have an impact he could never have foreseen.

Confronted with such an uncomfortable vision of his future legacy, Alfred Nobel decided to change his last will and testament. He allocated the vast majority of his fortune to establish five prizes, to be awarded each year to people who had conferred 'the greatest benefit on mankind'. The Nobel Prizes for physics, chemistry, medicine, literature and peace were born and have since become the world's most high-profile and well-respected awards for human achievement.

Two phases in life

How much thought have you given to the legacy you want *your* life to have? Now that you have reflected on your Inspiration Timeline in Part 2, are you heading in a direction that will leave you feeling inspired and fulfilled in the years you still have ahead of you?

In the last chapter, we explored the ways in which we can maintain our spirits from moment to moment and from day to day. Our focus will now lift to this higher level, to consider how we can stay more inspired over the course of our lives as a whole.

Alfred Nobel is not alone in having shifted his focus in the latter years of his life, hoping to leave an enduring, positive impact on the world. Many distinguished philosophers have noted the human tendency to reorientate our spiritual priorities as our lives unfold. A common theme is the idea that there tend to be two phases in life.

In the first, our focus is on achieving, winning, gaining and acquiring. We build our understanding of our own identity and establish a secure base for ourselves, financially and socially. In the second phase, our focus shifts to a search for greater meaning in our lives. Our priorities evolve from success to significance, from career to contributing, from gathering to scattering. If the first half of life is more about looking after our own selves, the second half is more about looking after others.

Not everyone makes this transition, and some, like Alfred Nobel, leave it until very late in their lives. For those with religious convictions, the implications extend well beyond our current existence on earth owing to a belief in some form of afterlife.

However, as the Dalai Lama and Archbishop Tutu pointed out in Chapter 3, the spiritual rewards available to us all, even just in this life, can be very significant. They are also fundamental to our nature as human beings: a sense of fulfilment that we have made the most of ourselves and who we have the potential to become; a confidence that we have lived out our own destiny to the fullest possible extent; and a belief that the world is a better place for having had us playing a part in it.

There is undoubtedly great wisdom contained in many of these ideas, but we are left with some nagging questions. Is it helpful to think about our lives in such a binary fashion, with a pre-enlightenment first phase and a post-enlightenment second phase? What are the implications for the way we should plan our lives and careers as leaders? And what happens if we face the possibility of our life being less long than we had expected?

A wake up call

Matt Dean is an experienced employment lawyer who set up his own consultancy business in 2003. Six years later, his life and those of his family and colleagues were turned upside down when he was diagnosed with throat cancer at the age of forty-four.

I have to declare a personal connection here. I first met Matt waiting in Reception as I arrived for my very first day at work with Unilever thirty years ago. I remember the moment clearly. There was something in Matt's charismatic manner, reinforced by a rather loud pair of socks, which suggested straight away he was going to be a colourful character. And so it proved. We struck up an immediate friendship that has lasted to this day.

After a couple of years toiling away as a marketing trainee, Matt soon came to the conclusion that he was in the wrong job. He left to study law and spent the next thirteen years working in a couple of prestigious City legal firms. He and his wife then moved on to set up their own company, byrne·dean, with the goal of helping companies deal with what they describe as 'the difficult stuff that happens when you employ people'.

Matt's cancer diagnosis in 2009 was followed by an aggressive course of chemo and radio therapies. Although the treatment made him very weak, it was successful. After six months he was told he was cancer free and over the next two years he slowly recovered physically to something like normal. Recently, however, a new malignant tumour was identified and Matt has just been through some serious surgery to replace part of his tongue.

'They can find no evidence of any cancer now,' Matt explains. 'But since the cancer returned, I must admit it's difficult not to think that it might come back again. It might be one year, it might be another seven – who knows? But I can't really believe the cancer's not going to come back at some point.'

What effect has his illness had on Matt's attitude to life? 'First time round, I'm told I was very close to dying,' he recalls. 'The more I came to appreciate that fact, the more strongly I felt that I wanted to do something important with the rest of my life.'

Despite his best intentions, however, Matt feels he hadn't made as much progress as he would have liked by the time the cancer reappeared. 'I was certainly not satisfied up to that moment,' he confides. 'You just carry on getting back to normal and doing the day-to-day stuff. Now I've had the second warning, I'm determined to make sure that I am using every day going forward to do something positive and meaningful. I can't ignore it anymore.'

A new drive for meaning

When Matt set up his own business, the first of the core values he defined for the company was *making a difference*. 'Our focus as a team is on creating better workplaces – that's what we care about. But I feel a frustration that we've not done enough of what we set out to do,' he admits.

'We work for big organisations, especially in financial services. If I'm honest the role we have played has often been helping them give their people risk-based messages: "Don't do this, don't do that!" The focus has been on making sure their employees avoid getting into legal difficulties over things like harassment, discrimination and bullying.'

'While this work has its place, the bigger, more important opportunity is in driving a *positive* agenda,' he continues. 'I want people to take responsibility for driving *improvements* in their bit of the workplace – increasing their leadership, being accountable. That's massively powerful. That's the agenda I want to drive.'

Matt also has a different, broader objective to capitalize on the experience that the cancer has given him. 'I'm absolutely clear I want to use the insight and wisdom that has come from going through this challenge,' he commits. 'I'm not sure quite what that looks like yet, but it might involve working with people in the NHS or Macmillan – something like that.'

Part of the insight Matt wants to share relates to a change that has taken place in his sense of identity. 'In essence, I think most people have a work self and a home self,' he explains. 'I decided that I would only ever have one self going forward. As an example, from the beginning I have been very open and honest with my clients and everyone I work with about my illness. A lot of people with cancer are scared about disclosing it at work, but I've actually found people have come back with an extremely positive, human reaction to the vulnerability I've shown.'

However, it is Matt's perspective on the value of his relationships with his family, friends and colleagues that has gone through the most significant transformation. 'The central learning for me is that there's only one thing that matters in the end, and that's love,' Matt avows.

His experience reinforces dramatically, once again, the vital importance of our intrinsic motivation to connect with other people in caring, committed relationships. 'I've spent so much of my time focused on work and I know I've not always been the easiest person to live with,' he confesses. 'It's hugely important to me now that I put my relationships with my wife and my three boys first and make them as positive as I possibly can.'

'With the first cancer, I did get to the point when I understood that I might actually die. I think you have to do that if you're going to get through the thing. You have to face your own mortality; we come from dust and we return to dust. And I got to the point when I was ok with that – I accepted it,' Matt reveals. 'That was only possible because I realized how privileged I've been, based on how much love I've been given and how much love I have given. Once you grasp that, you can move forward.'

'I have never had a negative experience, either inside or outside work, when I've behaved like a human being who loves people,' he concludes. 'As individuals, we come and go, but the love we give and receive is the one thing that survives. It's what matters most.'

Finding meaning later in life

Matt Dean's account of his battle with cancer is both moving and enlightening. Like Alfred Nobel before him, the reality of being confronted by his own mortality triggered a fundamental reassessment of his goals and priorities in life. For both men, the outcome was a resolve to place greater emphasis on their relationships with others and the positive impact they make with their lives.

Let us hope it never happens, but what impact do you think a diagnosis similar to the one given to Matt would have on *your* attitude to life? How would it shift your perspectives on your Inspiration Timeline – the extent to which you feel fulfilled by what you have achieved so far, enjoy what you are doing today and feel inspired by your future direction and purpose?

It is not always necessary to have to face the end of our life before we make a similar recalibration of our priorities. We learned of another common trigger for this kind of illumination back in Chapter 2 in the stories of Martin George and Arianna Huffington. As they both illustrated, leaders often reconsider their motivations once they have achieved career and material success, only to find them less fulfilling than they had expected.

A realization like this in mid-life raises many searching questions, particularly since at this stage we have time on our side to actually do something about it. For some leaders, the drive will remain undiminished to maximize their influence by fulfilling positions at the highest possible levels within their organizations. For others, a more varied portfolio of roles might become preferable, enabling them to balance their professional interests with other charitable or leisure pursuits.

These personal considerations are made even more important by the fact that so many of us will actually be leading much *longer* lives in the future. If current trends in life expectancy continue, today's sixty-year-olds have a 50 per cent chance of living till they are at least ninety. If you are currently forty, you have an equally high chance of living past ninety-five.

After all we have said about the value of time, a longer life can be seen as a priceless gift. But only if we find ways to spend the years ahead of us on our Inspiration Timeline wisely. No one wants to live through a forty-year retirement without the money, health or social network necessary to enjoy it.

How do we approach this challenge if the drive to acquire wealth, status and power that often underpins the earlier years of our career becomes less central to our motivation? How can we find the inspiration to embrace the later stages of our life with passion, excitement and wonder?

The solution surely lies in giving greater priority to the three intrinsic motivations that we introduced in Chapter 2. By channelling our energy into activities that play to our *passions*, that utilize and stretch our *talents* and that allow us to express our *values*, we have the potential to live an inspired life for as long as we desire.

Turning a city into a garden

Anyone who has driven from Changi Airport into Singapore city in the past five years cannot fail to have seen the spectacular Gardens by the Bay. Based on 100 hectares of reclaimed land at the city's heart, the Gardens is a dramatic showpiece of horticulture and garden artistry designed to bring alive the wonders of the plant kingdom.

The Gardens is the brainchild of Dr. Kiat Tan, a man who saw the project through late in life *after* he had supposedly retired. 'What does retirement mean?' he asks. 'I think one should always have a life that has some meaning. You should be able to give back whatever you have taken from the world from your existence. It's a matter of payback for what you have been blessed with.'

Dr Tan's love of botany was sparked at an early age by his mother's passion as an orchid breeder. He went on to study the subject at university in the United States in the late 1960s, before returning to Singapore as assistant commissioner in the country's Parks and Recreation Department.

'My dream was always to discover new types of plants that I thought were wonderful and to find a way to share these and tell their stories to as many people as I could,' he reflects. 'I realized that many people in Singapore just didn't have the opportunities I'd had to travel around the world, so that gave me a purpose.'

Over the course of his earlier career, Dr Tan played a central role in what became known as the greenification of Singapore. This involved softening up the landscape by planting trees and shrubs alongside the city's roads and drainage reserves. Inspired by the role that Central Park had played in New York, a hierarchy of different parks was also developed to provide 'green lungs' for the local community.

The transformation of Singapore into The Garden City was an ambitious and highly creative process. 'We had a unique opportunity to add more species and interest into the mix,' Dr Tan recalls. 'Why limit ourselves? We even introduced the tiering of vegetation you find in forests to create a more naturalistic kind of landscaping.'

Dr Tan went on to become the director of the Singapore Botanic Gardens. When this body merged with the Parks and Recreation Department to form the National Parks Board, he became the board's founding CEO. But when the time finally came to retire, he had other plans.

'The idea for Gardens by the Bay was conceived and proposed to the government's Cabinet in 2004. The project broke ground in 2007 and opened to the public in 2012. Very fast!' he laughs.

'I think the most gratifying part of it has been seeing just how many people have come to view the gardens. I was very fortunate to be able to build the two domes, like the ones at the Eden Project. They have shielded people from our inclement weather, and they also meant I could grow a range of plants that people don't normally see in Singapore.'

Based on his extraordinary experience, what advice would Dr Tan give to other leaders about how to find such passion and inspiration over the full course of their lives?

'I think some of it may come from just living and becoming more mature, but you must *know yourself*. You have to be true to what you consider is *you*,' he urges. 'If you can identify and focus on what truly motivates you, there need be no effort or sacrifice in achieving the goals you have.'

'For me, as I look around, there are just so many wonders in this world,' he enthuses. 'Wherever you go, the inter-relationship between plants and animal life. Things living up in the trees, things living down on the ground. Amazing! There's no end to it. How can you not constantly be stimulated by life?'

A new shape to life

Dr Kiat Tan's decision to keep working well beyond his designated retirement age is not unusual these days. In their book *The 100-Year Life*, Lynda Gratton and Andrew Scott paint a fascinating picture of what people's lives will begin to look like as they adjust to the prospect of living longer.

The three traditional life stages prevalent in the twentieth century – education/career/retirement – are already beginning to blur. Multi-stage lives are set to become more common, with people engaged in a broader and less predictable variety of jobs and activities at different times. We might have several careers, rather than just one, and we are increasingly likely to retrain and reinvent ourselves as our lives play out.

Just as old age will change as people work well into their seventies and eighties, so too will being young. Many people leaving university today are already behaving differently from previous generations, looking to explore and experiment before making commitments to specific career choices.

One of the big benefits of this approach is that it gives young people the opportunity to find out more about themselves, their interests and their talents at an earlier stage in their lives. Dr Tan is not alone in suggesting that knowing yourself is something that takes time and experience. However, there is evidence to suggest that some young people are learning how to live inspired lives a lot earlier and more successfully than some of their elders might think.

The idea shared earlier that you have to wait until the second half of life before being able to reach 'enlightenment' is certainly challenged by the wisdom, spirit and impact demonstrated by individuals like Sarah Ellis.

A young portfolio career

Sarah fizzes with energy as she tells me about all the things she is currently doing with her life. Approaching her mid-thirties, Sarah Ellis leads a team of twenty-five people in her role as head of Marketing Strategy at Sainsbury's. She works part-time and devotes the rest of her working week to two other enterprises she founded herself.

The first is Amazing If, a company that provides courses, content and coaching to help people lead happy careers. The other is Inspire, a charity that creates learning opportunities for people in the marketing industry. The money raised from these experiences is then used to support marketing apprenticeships for people from disadvantaged backgrounds.

How on earth does she find the time to do it all? 'The number one thing is I don't do it all by myself!' she laughs. 'I have a brilliant business partner and a group of very smart volunteers who put in just as much energy and enthusiasm as I do.'

'You certainly have to be very organized and prioritize your time carefully,' she continues. 'It's so worth it though. I love the portfolio nature of what I do – the variety, the mix. I find the whole definitely bigger than the sum of the parts.'

Over the course of her career so far, Sarah has been fastidious in her efforts to learn about and be guided by her intrinsic motivations. 'I've thought hard about what I was really great at and what I really enjoyed; what I wanted to be spending my time doing every day,' she explains.

'I see each job, each experience I have as a constant process of discovery. I think you can become very self-aware from an early age if you have the right mindset. As I've learned what matters to me, I have just kept making choices that have gradually taken me closer and closer to the things I love.'

Sarah's thirst for variety and learning seems boundless. 'My favourite piece of career advice is to never live the same year twice,' she smiles. 'I'm much less worried these days about the next job and the job after that. I've changed the way I think about what it means to be progressing. It's less about going down the traditional career paths and more about exploring what you enjoy and seeing where that takes you. I like the idea of people having squiggly careers!'

Discovering inspiration early in life

Given the role she plays in guiding young people in their career decisions, Sarah is particularly well placed to advise on how they might find ways to live more inspired lives.

'It can be extremely unhelpful and patronizing to be told that you need more experience before you can really know what you want to do or what you're good at,' Sarah observes. 'Of course experience is useful, but there are definitely ways you can set out to learn about yourself very quickly.'

'There's also nothing more frustrating or demotivating than just telling this new generation to do what they love and to hell with the consequences,' she asserts. 'People have got rent to pay and if you're in a city, it's incredibly expensive. The issue they need help with is how they can find a career they enjoy and that also pays the bills.'

'For me, the secret lies in using every little experience as a learning opportunity. We have to bring a growth mindset to our lives – exploring, reflecting, seeking feedback from people continually,' Sarah urges. 'It's about breaking things down into lots of incremental, small-scale actions rather than just searching for big transformational steps.'

'We need to see ourselves as works-in-progress – exploring our strengths, our values and our interests all the time,' Sarah concludes. 'I don't think it matters whether you're 21 or 51, life is all about looking to learn and reflecting on the experiences we go through. That's ultimately where our inspiration will come from.'

And with this insight, Sarah Ellis helps bring us back full circle to where we started the book in Chapter 1 and the alchemy of inspiration. It seems that no matter where we are along life's journey, the elements that have the potential to inspire us remain the same.

What is it that truly motivates us? Are we bringing the right positive and learning-orientated mindsets? Are we experiencing life and all of its potential triggers to the full?

Our answers to these fundamental, life-shaping questions will evolve as we progress on our journey through time. But that makes it all the more important that we keep asking ourselves the questions.

Our drive to learn and to grow will never diminish. The more we can maximize and multiply ourselves, the more significant and fulfilling our lives will become. That is what makes living so exciting. And it is ultimately what makes being a leader so inspiring.

INSPIRATION OVER A LIFETIME: IN SUMMARY…

- Our priorities tend to evolve as we get older, with a shift from success to significance, from career to contributing, from gathering to scattering.

- As our focus moves from looking after our own selves to looking after others, the spiritual rewards available to us are fundamental to our human nature.

- Seeing life in terms of a pre-enlightenment first phase and a post-enlightenment second phase risks over-simplifying the spiritual progression we can go through as our lives play out.

- As our life expectancy increases, people are set to lead multi-stage lives during which they will engage in a broader and less predictable variety of jobs and activities.

- No matter what stage we have reached on our journey through life, the elements that have the potential to inspire us remain the same: our motivations, our mindsets and our triggers.

- By channelling our energy into activities that we love being involved in, that we find challenging and that we believe have meaning and value beyond ourselves, we have the potential to live an inspired life whatever age we may be.

REFLECTIONS 11: MY FUTURE LIFE

When your life comes to an end at some point in the future …

What would you like to have done?

What words would you like people to use to describe the kind of person you have been?

Looking back at your personal purpose in Chapter 6, what kind of impact would you like to have made in the world?

What can you do to start making sure these desires come true?

Today　　　　　*This month*　　　　　*This year*

IF YOUR ACTIONS INSPIRE OTHERS TO
DREAM MORE, LEARN MORE, DO MORE AND
BECOME MORE, YOU ARE A LEADER.

JOHN QUINCY ADAMS

12

MAINTAIN	
10	Sources of Resilience
11	Inspiration over a Lifetime
12	Inspiring Others

Back at the very start of the book, we began with Peter Drucker's wise observation that the first and foremost job of any leader is to find ways to manage their own energy. In the eleven chapters since, we have explored what this means in practice, focusing on the approaches we can take to discover, experience and maintain our own inspiration over time.

However, Dr Drucker's advice did not end there. He went on to say that leaders must then *orchestrate the energy of those around them*. In the previous chapter, we heard from Sarah Ellis that the only way she manages to have the impact she does as a leader is because 'other people put in just as much energy and enthusiasm as I do'.

In this concluding chapter, we will consider how leaders can 'maximize and multiply' their influence by getting better at *inspiring others*. And what better way to approach this challenge than by reflecting on all we have learned about how we find that same inspiration ourselves.

As you have progressed through the book, you will no doubt have generated your own insights about how you can feel more inspired, more of the time. This is now your opportunity to consider the potential implications for the way you can help instil the same passion, commitment and resilience in the hearts and minds of the people you are leading.

To help stimulate your thinking, I will highlight six lessons that have stood out for me as I have reflected back on the many conversations I have had with leaders. Why six? For no other reason than there happened to be six that I felt were most important to share!

Inspiration is infectious. The more inspired we feel personally, the more we will be able to help generate that same spirit in others. And the better we do that, the more our inspired colleagues will play a role in maintaining our own inspiration as leaders in return.

Here are some ideas to help you get the ball rolling ...

1. Embrace your personal influence

We have learned that one of the most important triggers for our inspiration is the encounters we have with other people.

Moreover, the people who typically have more impact on our spirit than any other are the ones we work for – our bosses.

If we reorientate the way we consider this, it confronts us with a challenging question. What impact are *we* having on the people we are leading currently? When your own colleagues look back on their careers, will they remember you as a role model who inspired them in *positive* ways?

The first step in getting better at inspiring others is simply to recognize the power of the influence we have on the people around us. The more senior we get, the more this responsibility grows. The impact of our behaviour, and the ripples it sends throughout the organization, is often a great deal more significant than we appreciate.

Instead of letting our minds focus on the pressures we are under and the concerns we may be feeling about ourselves, we need to turn our attention instead to think more about the role we are playing in managing the energy of others. As leaders, we are 'always on', whether we like it or not. People are constantly watching us to pick up the signs from what we say and do, and just as importantly, what we don't say and don't do.

One man who knew how to use his personal presence brilliantly in this way was Nelson Mandela. Niall FitzGerald has chaired the Nelson Mandela Legacy Trust and tells the story of a lunch meeting he had with the great man at his house in Sussex back in 2005.

'We had two young gardeners at the time, both in their early 20s,' Niall recalls. 'There was a lot of security in the lead up to the visit, but I explained to these guys just beforehand who was about to arrive. I suggested that if they wanted to see Mr Mandela close up, they could come and stand next to a van by the entrance.'

The official cavalcade duly arrived. Nelson Mandela emerged and began walking up towards the house. Niall continues with the story: 'As he approached the place where the gardeners were standing, he stopped and asked: "Are you the two boys who have made this beautiful garden?" He stood smiling and nodding as they responded and then, looking each of them in the eye, he said simply: "Thank you." And then he walked on.'

'I promise you, these two guys, they grew twelve feet tall in front of my very eyes!' Niall laughs. 'They will go to their graves with that ten-second encounter being one of the most inspirational things they ever experienced.'

'That was Nelson Mandela's extraordinary talent,' Niall observes. 'He would always pick out the people who would be *assumed* as the least important – the receptionist, the photographer, in this case the gardeners – and he'd make them the first people he'd acknowledge and talk to. He was giving a signal – everyone here is important to me, everybody here is of value. That was part of his genius as a leader.'

Nelson Mandela may be a tough role model to match up to, but there is a lesson in this story for us all. What are the signals *we* want to give out to the people we meet and work with? How are we using *our* presence to impact the energy of those around us? Becoming more mindful of the influence we can have is the first place to start if we want to get better at inspiring others.

2. Involve people in your purpose …
and in you as their leader

To be inspired means being motivated to do, or to be, certain positive things as we look to the future. It stands to reason, then, that if we are to help others find inspiration, we have to help them discover what they feel excited about working towards.

This lesson is one that I learned myself in the early years of leading Brand Learning with my partner, Mhairi McEwan. We both had a strong intuitive sense of the kind of business we were trying to create. As we brought on board some impressive, senior colleagues to join us, I remember doing all I could to engage with them personally and to motivate them as individuals.

Mhairi and I soon discovered, though, that the sense of purpose we both shared so deeply, was not being felt to the same extent by the others. The breakthrough in our team spirit came when we ran a session in which we confronted and acknowledged the dynamics that were going on between us as a group. Each person was then invited to reflect on their own personal passions and values and we used these as a springboard to create a new *shared* mission and vision for the company. We painted a picture of the future together that we all felt involved in and had some ownership for.

Leadership coach Steve Radcliffe talks about the importance of leaders building within their team 'a shared sense of being up to something together'. To be clear, this does not mean imposing our own leadership purpose on others. Neither does it mean abrogating responsibility and leaving it to the team to come up with something themselves.

A leader must bring their own spirit of excitement, resolve, involvement and meaning to help set the agenda in the first place. But by involving others in building on this, they can then develop a broader sense of purpose that the whole team feels passionate about and committed to. The process of co-creation is at least as important as the end result, as it plays such a central role in generating the spirit required.

However, leaders will be missing a trick if they leave it at that. Inspiring people by engaging them in a vision of the future is vital, but leaders have an opportunity to go one step further by encouraging people to engage with them personally too.

In recent years, I have been involved in several leadership team sessions when the leader has opened up to share something important about themselves with their colleagues. By talking about their values, beliefs and their personal stories in a spirit of authenticity and humility, leaders can quickly build a deep personal rapport with the other people in their team. They can also shift the dynamics within the team as a whole, as their disclosure is reciprocated by others and an atmosphere of trust begins to emerge.

Having been through the reflective exercises in this book, you should hopefully be clear about the most important elements that underpin your own leadership – your values, passions and talents; your leadership mindsets and beliefs. It is worth considering how you might share these, openly and honestly, with the people you are leading. By doing so, you have the potential to enthuse them not just with the inspiring prospect of the future you will create together, but also with the mutual understanding, belief and respect that lies at the heart of their relationship with you.

3. Care for people as individuals

Usain Bolt is a man who hasn't done a bad job at fulfilling his potential! His unprecedented feat of winning the sprint gold medals at three successive Olympic Games surely establishes him as the world's greatest ever athlete.

Kerris Bright has come to know Usain through his involvement in Virgin Media's advertising campaigns. Even she claims to run a little bit faster in the gym now that she's met him! I'm grateful to Kerris for posing some questions to Usain to discover how his coach, Glen Mills, has helped him find the inspiration to reach such incredible levels of performance.

'For me, if you're really going to get the best out of yourself, the key thing is you have to work hard,' Usain begins. 'You don't get to be an Olympic champion without *really* working hard. You have to push yourself to the ultimate limit. A lot of people try a bit and feel like: "Well… . I've done my best." But sometimes you have to push yourself to your absolute breaking point.'

So what role has 'Coach' Mills played in supporting these efforts? 'I think you need someone to help you sometimes,' Usain continues. 'Not always will you have the drive to go out and really give it your best. You always need that person in your corner, who knows who you are and knows the goals you're working towards; who wants to help you, to push you and lift you up.'

'When I'm dying in training or not feeling good, Coach Mills will say: "Listen, this is what you're working towards – you've got to step up, you've got to push on,"' Usain explains. 'He's not just a coach to me – we're friends. He's just so relaxing; I laugh so much around him. Coach Mills is like a father figure to me, a big role model. Throughout the years of being with him, he's taught me such a lot about life overall. That's why he's different, that's why our relationship works.'

All of us need support from others if we are to become all we are capable of becoming. As Usain Bolt has demonstrated so sensationally, it can make all the difference to have someone in your corner who understands you, someone committed to your success and who provides just the right blend of challenge and support to bring out the best in you.

Back in Chapter 3, Nihal Kaviratne advocated that this kind of relationship begins with the *care* a leader has for the people they are leading. Inspiring other people is not just about getting them to be impressed by you and what you do. It is about demonstrating your concern and interest in *them*, ensuring they feel respected, special and valued. It is clear from the reverential way in which Usain Bolt speaks about his coach that Glen Mills has done this job superbly.

Just as our own inspiration comes from tapping into our own values, passions and talents, so it is for the people we lead. We need to engage with them as individuals, helping them to better understand their own intrinsic motivations themselves and then working to create the conditions within which they can flourish.

This certainly does not mean that being a leader is about being soft. Coach Mills clearly gives Usain Bolt a hard time when he needs it. There will be times when tough conversations are required to address poor performance, in some cases to the extent of having to ask people to leave the team. But even the most difficult discussions can still be handled in a spirit of care, so that we help people maintain their dignity and self-respect at the times when they need it most.

4. Make the most of your place in time

In Part 2, we learned that the way we actually experience inspiration is determined by our perspective in relation to time. The Inspiration Timeline provides tremendous opportunities for leaders to be more proactive in managing the energy of the people in their immediate team and their organization more generally.

The importance of working with people to create a shared sense of purpose as they look to the future has already been highlighted. To remind us of an example, Patrick Spence described in Chapter 6 the Sonos team's mission to fill every home with music, and their vision to change the way people listen to music – one home at a time. He stressed how important these ideas are in bringing everyone together and creating a spirit of excitement about the opportunities ahead.

However, inspiration is not *only* about the future. Lisa Anson's Art of the Possible initiative at AstraZeneca, explained in Chapter 8, is a great case of celebrating past successes and using them to fuel belief and ambition throughout an organization. Finding ways to praise people's past efforts, to acknowledge important lessons and to thank people for their contributions are all ways of lifting confidence within a team. They will also help increase people's commitment to the cause and to you personally as their leader.

Perhaps the most important yet least appreciated form of inspiration is our enjoyment of the present. We can lift our spirits by thinking about what lies ahead, or by reflecting back on past achievements, but ultimately we only ever experience time in the present moment. If people aren't enjoying their work on a day-to-day basis, their energy is bound to flag.

It is therefore incumbent on leaders to ensure people enjoy a sense of autonomy in their roles, enabling them to channel their energy and talent into the activities they find most enjoyable and challenging. Leaders can also influence the spirit in which the work gets done, by managing the mindsets they bring and the way they show up in person. The more a team's culture is orientated around positivity, learning and fun, the more enjoyable even the most demanding tasks will become.

The busier life gets, the more difficult it can be to carve out the time we need to connect with ourselves and with each other. Yet, paradoxically, this space for personal mindfulness and building relationships becomes all the more important as the pressure we are under grows. Creating opportunities for people to step back and reflect on what they are doing and why they are doing it will certainly add to their enjoyment of the present. Importantly, it will also increase the chances of them experiencing illumination, the fourth and final form of inspiration.

Leaders need to think about the various triggers they can use to help their people discover enlightening new insights. Other tactics include arranging encounters with inspiring people or invigorating experiences that broaden people's awareness of life outside their organization. The main goal is to stimulate shifts in people's perspectives on the world, their jobs and their own selves. The potential results will not just be creative new ideas about the work they do, but also injections of new spirit in the way they do it.

5. Seek genuine feedback from others

One of the most potent sources of illumination for leaders themselves is the feedback they receive about their leadership from the people they are leading. Much as we might desire to bring inspiration to those we work with, whether we actually do or not is a different matter. The impact we intend to have on people is rarely the same as the impact that is actually felt by them. And the only way of finding that out is to discover their opinion.

It requires a fair degree of personal strength and self-confidence to open up to people in this way. We all have fears about our weaknesses and faults, so many leaders steer clear of asking for feedback of this type to avoid hearing things they might not like.

Indeed, even those that do ask will rarely obtain honest feedback. Most people feel inhibited in what they say to their boss. In some cases they might not want to hurt their feelings, but more often they will simply fear the potential consequences on their career prospects and job security.

The challenge facing leaders is therefore to seek feedback from their teams in a true spirit of openness and enquiry. In order to create the safe environment necessary, leaders need to show some personal vulnerability and a genuine willingness to hear about and accept the concerns their colleagues might raise.

Niall FitzGerald has a characteristically insightful point of view on this topic. 'I can't stress enough the importance of authenticity and of showing people who you really are, with all your vulnerabilities. The fact is that you can't be a leader without having followers. Followers want to help. They want to follow someone they can relate to, not some icon of perfection.'

Once again we return to the importance of the relationship between a leader and the people they lead. One of the most influential ways of making that relationship a deeper and more inspiring one is to talk with people about the relationship itself, seeking insight into how things are working from each other's perspective.

I am grateful to a coaching colleague and friend, Anni Townend, for introducing me to a very practical way of handling this type of conversation. It starts with each person affirming upfront that the feedback they are seeking to give and receive is focused on *impact* – their *felt* experience of each other. They also commit that this feedback will be given in a positive spirit of commitment to each other's success.

The conversation then goes through four stages in which each person takes their turn in asking the other person the questions below. To be clear, each person gives their feedback on the same question at each stage, before moving on together to the next round of the conversation.

1 *Acknowledge*: What *do* you get from me that you *do* want from me? How does that make you feel?

2 *Request*: What *don't* you get from me that you *do* want from me? How does that make you feel?

3 *Challenge*: What *do* you get from me that you *don't* want from me? How does that make you feel?

4 *Guide*: What is the single most important piece of encouragement you can give me that will help me be even more inspiring?

I have used this technique with numerous leaders and their teams and I can vouch for its power. Give it a go yourself. By opening up genuine two-way feedback conversations, leaders can step change their own self-awareness and also the quality of their relationships with their colleagues.

6. Foster a more balanced culture of leadership

As I have reflected back on the overall line of argument laid out in this book, I am conscious there is one big unanswered question that needs to be addressed before closing.

I have suggested that given the volatile nature of the world today, strong leadership has never been more important. But that same volatility is also putting greater pressure on leaders than ever before. It is for this reason that leadership inspiration is so vital.

We have learned that this inspiration is fuelled by leaders getting involved in work that they have a passion for, that draws on and challenges their talents, and that enables them to stand up for the core values they believe in.

However, the issue is this. What if, despite all these efforts, the difficulties and stresses involved in being a leader are simply too intense for most people to bear? What if potentially great leaders opt instead for an easier life with less responsibility and public scrutiny?

This is not a hypothetical question. Recent press reports in the UK have highlighted the dearth of CEOs in National Health Service trusts and head teachers in schools. Research also suggests that many women lack the desire to step up into the most senior roles in corporate organizations, owing to the cultural expectations surrounding many of these positions.

This brings us to the sixth and final call to action for leaders. We need to find opportunities to shift the way in which the nature of leadership itself is understood and experienced going forward. A more balanced approach is required in which leaders fulfil the responsibilities they have to people in their organizations, and to society more broadly, with integrity and authenticity. In return, they should be able to live lives in which the professional demands they face can realistically be met alongside their need for personal enjoyment and well-being.

This balance has a number of dimensions. Leaders themselves must balance their own self-interest with the interests of others. They need to embrace the benefits of balancing their extrinsic desire for money, status and power with their more intrinsic motivations to explore, learn and build caring relationships. They must seek to balance the emphasis on intellectual and physical energy in their organizations, by giving greater support to people's emotional and spiritual energy.

In return, the prevailing expectations we have of our leaders must be moderated too. Leaders are only human and will not always cope faultlessly or single-handedly with everything the world might throw at them. We need to recognize that effective leadership increasingly requires a distributed team effort, rather than one heroic person who we rely upon to work all the hours and solve all the problems.

Today's leaders have a central role to play in influencing the way this cultural development takes place. They have the opportunity to role model new ways of leading that will create more inspiring opportunities for their potential successors. By having the strength and humility to be their true selves at work, rather than hiding behind a professional mask, they can give other people the licence to do the same. By upholding the positive aspects of human nature, they can infuse their organizations with a spirit of hope, confidence, enthusiasm and trust.

Perhaps the most important balance needed is in the way leaders choose the values that underpin what they are leading *for*. As Claire Chiang urged in Chapter 1, leaders must raise their game to give greater emphasis to the human values that bring people together, rather than drive them apart; values that encourage inclusivity and tolerance, rather than discrimination and conflict.

Championing this spirit of humanity will not only provide a deep and potent source of inspiration for today's leaders. It will also be invaluable in inspiring the next generation too – the new leaders we depend upon to create an exciting, prosperous and peaceful world as we head into the future.

INSPIRING OTHERS: IN SUMMARY...

- Our understanding of the way we are inspired personally provides us with invaluable insight to help us instil the same passion, commitment and resilience in the hearts and minds of the people we are leading.

- There are six useful lessons to bear in mind as you seek to inspire other people:

    1 Embrace your personal influence

    2 Involve others in your purpose ... and in you as their leader

    3 Care for people as individuals

    4 Make the most of your place in time

    5 Seek genuine feedback from others

    6 Foster a more balanced culture of leadership

REFLECTIONS 12: INSPIRING OTHERS

What are your most important insights into how you can personally be more inspired as a leader?

What are the implications for the way you will now seek to inspire other people?

I wish you every success as you seek to put into practice all the ideas and commitments you have generated here and in the previous reflective exercises.

ACKNOWLEDGEMENTS

I have referred a number of times in the pages of this book to how powerful the feeling of gratitude can be. I am certainly experiencing that now as I reflect on the amazing support I have had from so many people during the journey to getting it published.

First, I would like to thank Steve Walker and Sam Ellis who have been with me every step of the way over the past few months. I am deeply grateful for the generous gift of their time and their thoughtful advice, encouragement and challenge. I must also acknowledge the pivotal input of Liz Cox at a crucial moment during the book's development.

I am indebted to the many colleagues and friends who have either helped connect me to the people I have interviewed or provided feedback on the book text as it has emerged. Thank you also to the team at Bloomsbury for their publishing support, to Stacy Sheridan for her administrative help, and to Rodney Minter-Brown and Tandy and Anton van Schalkwyk for all their work on graphics, visuals and website development.

The idea for the book first emerged as I was studying for an MSc in Coaching & Behaviour Change at Henley Business

School, so thank you to all who taught me so much there – notably Alison Hardingham, Patricia Riddell, Patricia Bossons, Nigel Spink and my research supervisor Jeremy Cross.

I would also like to take this opportunity to express my sincere gratitude to Mhairi McEwan and my other colleagues at Brand Learning. Special mention must be made of Ana Maria Santos, Jill Hughes, Michele McGrath,   Nevine El-Warraky and the other Brand Learning partners and shareholders, all of whom have made an incredible contribution to our success. It has been such a pleasure working with them and so many other great people in our team over the years. I particularly appreciate the support they have given me recently as I have shifted my professional focus towards leadership development and coaching.

That shift was triggered in large part by the inspiration I have experienced myself working so closely with Steve Radcliffe on The Marketing Society's International Marketing Leaders Programme. Thank you so much to Hugh Burkitt for offering me the opportunity to be involved in the first place, and to Steve and his colleague Anni Townend for the coaching and encouragement they have given me since.

Most important of all, I must thank my family for all their love and support – my parents Ann and Derek, my brothers David and Peter, and my children Suzie and Jonnie. My dear wife Jacqui has always been a wonderful source of wisdom, emotional support and patient listening, but never has this been of more value than in the past few months. The most common phrase used recently in the Bird household has been, 'When the book is finished…'. Well, I am pleased to say the book *is* finally finished and normal life can now resume!

REFERENCES

The full details of the literature I have used to inform the book are listed below. The sources I recommend as being of particular value are highlighted with an * and written in bold.

Introduction

Evans, J. (2009). *Inspirational Presence: The Art of Transformational Leadership.* New York: Morgan James.

* **Heimans, J. and Timms, H. (2014). Understanding 'New Power'. *Harvard Business Review*, December 2014.**

Horney, N., Passmore, B. and O'Shea, T. (2010). Leadership agility: A business imperative for a VUCA world. *People & Strategy*, 33(4), pp. 32–8.

Kotter, J. (2001). What leaders really do. *Harvard Business Review*, December 2001.

Kwoh, L. (2013). When the CEO burns out. *Wall Street Journal*, 7 May 2013.

McNulty, E. (2015). Leading in an increasingly VUCA world. *Strategy+Business*, www.strategy-business.com/blog

Roche, M. (2013). Leader's life aspirations and job burnout: A self-determination theory approach. *Leadership & Organization Development Journal*, 34(6), pp. 515–31.

Chapter 1: The alchemy of inspiration

Baumeister, R. F. (2011). Self and identity: A brief overview of what they are, what they do, and how they work, *Annals of the New York Academy of Sciences*, Issue: Perspectives on the Self.

Bossons, P., Riddell, P. and Sartain, D. (2015) *The Neuroscience of Leadership Coaching*, London: Bloomsbury.

Lee, G. (2003). *Leadership Coaching*. London, UK: CIPD.

Pless, N. M. and Maak, T. (2011). Values, authenticity and responsible leadership. *Journal of Business Ethics*, 98, pp. 15–23.

* **Thrash, T. M. and Elliot, A. J. (2003). Inspiration as a psychological construct. *Journal of Personality and Social Psychology*, 84(4), pp. 871–89.**

Chapter 2: Inner motivations

Brosch, T., and Sander, D. (2014). Appraising value: The role of universal core values and emotions in decision-making. *Cortex*, 9, pp. 10–12.

Chan, K. Y. and Drasgow, F. (2001). Toward a theory of individual differences and leadership: understanding the motivation to lead. *The Journal of Applied Psychology*. 86(3), pp. 481–98.

Elliot, A. J. and Covington, M. V. (2001). Approach and avoidance. *Educational Psychology Review*, 13(2), pp. 73–92.

George, B. and Sims, P. (2007). *True North: Discover Your Authentic Leadership*. San Francisco, CA: Jossey-Bass.

Di Domenico, S. I. and Ryan, R. M. (2017). The emerging neuroscience of intrinsic motivation. *Frontiers in Human Neuroscience*, March 2017, Volume 11, Article 145.

* **Huffington, A. (2014). *Thrive: The Third Metric to Redefining Success and Creating a Happier Life*. Kindle edition: Virgin Digital.**

Isaac, R. G., Zerbe, W. J. and Pitt, D. C. (2001). Leadership and motivation: The effective application of expectancy theory. *Journal of Managerial Issues*, 13(2), pp. 212–26.

Lawrence, P. and Nohria, N. (2007) *Driven: How Human Nature Shapes Our Choices*. Kindle edition: Jossey-Bass.

Lorsch, J. (2010). The Pay Problem, *Harvard Magazine*, May–June 2010.

Locke, E. A. (1991). The motivation sequence, the motivation hub, and the motivation core. *Organizational Behavior and Human Decision Processes*, 50(2), pp. 288–99.

Maslow, A. H. (1970). *Motivation and Personality*, 3rd edn, Pearson.

Maccoby, M. (2004). Narcissistic leaders: The incredible pros and the inevitable cons. *Harvard Business Review*, January 2004.

McClelland, D. C. and Boyatzis, R. E. (1982). Leadership motive pattern and long-term success in management. *Journal of Applied Psychology*, 67(6), pp. 737–43.

Parsons, G. D. and Pascale, R. T. (2007). Crisis at the summit. *Harvard Business Review*, March 2007.

* **Robinson, K. (2013). *Finding Your Element: How to Discover your Talents and Passions*. Kindle edition: Penguin**.

Ryan, R. and Deci, E. (2000). Intrinsic and extrinsic motivations: Classic definitions and new directions. *Contemporary Educational Psychology*, 25(1), pp. 54–67.

Ryan, R. and Deci, E (2001). On happiness and human potentials: A review of research on hedonic and eudaimonic well-being. *Annual Review of Psychology*, 52, pp. 141–66.

* **Ryan, R. and Deci, E. (2017). *Self-Determination Theory: Basic Psychological needs in Motivation, Development and Wellness*. Kindle edition: Guilford Press**.

Sachau, D. (2015). Work Motivation. *Salem Encyclopedia of Health*, January 2015.

Schwartz, S. H. (1992). Universals in the content and structure of values: Theoretical advances and empirical tests in 20 countries. *Advances in Experimental Social Psychology*, 25(C), pp. 1–65.

Chapter 3: Engaging mindsets

* **Abrams, D., Lama, Dalai and Tutu, D. (2016). *The Book of Joy*. London: Penguin Random House**.

Frankl, V. (1946). *Man's Search for Meaning*. Kindle edition: Random House.

Gopalakrishnan, R. (2016). *Six Lenses: Vignettes of Success, Career and Relationships*. New Delhi: Rupa.

Judge, T. A., Bono, J. E., Ilies, R. and Gerhardt, M. W. (2002). Personality and leadership: A qualitative and quantitative review. *The Journal of Applied Psychology*, 87(4), pp. 765–80.

Lyubomirsky, S. (2007). *The How of Happiness*. London: Piatkus.

Peck, M. S. (1978) *The Road Less Travelled*. Kindle edition: Rider.

Nakamura, J. and Csikszentmihalyi, M. (2003). The construction of meaning through vital engagement. In C. L. M. Keyes and J. Haidt (eds), *Flourishing: Positive Psychology and the Life Well Lived*. Washington, DC: American Psychological Association, pp. 83–104.

Chapter 4: External triggers

Bennis, W. G. and Thomas, R. J. (2002). Crucibles of leadership. *Harvard Business Review*, September 2002.

* **Swain, B. (2016). Successful leaders know what made them who they are. *Harvard Business Review*, September 2016**.

Thrash, T. M. and Elliot, A. J. (2004). Inspiration: Core characteristics, component processes, antecedents, and function. *Journal of Personality and Social Psychology*, 87(6), pp. 957–73.

Yalom, I. D. (2008). *Staring at the Sun*. Kindle edition: Hatchette Digital.

Chapter 5: The inspiration timeline

Seligman, M., Railton, P., Baumeister, R. and Sripada C. (2013). Navigating into the future or driven by the past. *Perspectives on Psychological Science*, 8, p. 119.

Chapter 6: Fuelled by purpose

Bird, A. and McEwan, M. (2012). *The Growth Drivers*. Chichester, UK: Wiley.

Craig, N. and Snook, S. A. (2014). From purpose to impact. *Harvard Business Review*, May 2014.

Heifetz, R., Grashow, A. and Linsky, M. (2009). Stay connected to your purposes. In *The Practice of Adaptive Leadership*, Boston, MA: Harvard Business Press.

* **Pink, D. H. (2009). *Drive: The Surprising Truth About What Motivates Us*. New York: Riverhead Books**.

* **Radcliffe, S. (2012). *Leadership Plain and Simple*. Harlow: Pearson**.

Ray, M. (2004). *The Highest Goal: The Secret that Sustains you in Every Moment*. Oakland, CA: Berret-Koehler.

Sinek, S. (2011). *Start With Why: How Leaders Inspire Everyone to Take Action*. Kindle edition: Penguin.

Chapter 7: Alive with enjoyment

Branson, R. (2015). *My Tips for Happiness*, 29 July 2015: www.virgin.com/richard-branson/my-tips-for-happiness

Carroll, M. (2011). *The Mindful Leader*. Boston, MA: Trumpeter.

* **Csikszentmihalyi, M. (2002). *Flow: The Psychology of Happiness*. Kindle edition: Rider**.

Giannachi, G. and Luckhurst, M. (1999). Declan Donnellan, in *On Directing*. London: Faber & Faber.

Smith, A. C. (2008). The neuroscience of spirituality in organisations. *Journal of Management, Spirituality & Religion*, 5, pp. 1, 3–28.

Chapter 8: Fulfilled by achievement

* **Dweck, C. (2012). *Mindset: Changing the Way you Think to Fulfil your Potential*. London: Random House**.

Katzenbach, J. R. (2006). Motivation beyond money: Learning from peak performers. *Leader To Leader*, Summer 2006.

McClelland, D. C. (1985). *Human Motivation*. Cambridge, UK: Cambridge University Press.

Molden, D. and Dweck, C. (2000). Meaning and motivation, in C. Sansone and J. M. Harackiewicz (eds), *Intrinsic and Extrinsic Motivation*, San Diego, CA: Academic Press, pp. 131–59.

O'Connell, P. (2016). *The Battle*. Kindle edition: Penguin.

Paglis, L. L. (2010). Leadership self-efficacy: Research findings and practical applications. *Journal of Management Development*, 29(9), pp. 771–82.

Seppala, E. (2013). The Compassionate Mind. Association for Psychological Science, May/June 2013.

Weiner, B. (1985). An attributional theory of achievement motivation and emotion. *Psychological Review*, 92(4), pp. 548–73.

Chapter 9: Enriched with illumination

Oleynick, V. C., Thrash, T. M., Lefew, M. C., Moldovan, E. G., Kieffaber, P. D. and Baas, M. (2014). The scientific study of inspiration in the creative process: challenges and opportunities. *Frontiers in Human Neuroscience*, 8, p. (436).

* **Rooke, D. and Torbert, W. R. (2005). Seven transformations of leadership. *Harvard Business Review*, April 2005.**

Chapter 10: Sources of resilience

Coutu, D. (2002). How resilience works. *Harvard Business Review*, May 2012.

Dannatt, R. (2010) *Leading From The Front*. Kindle edition: Transworld Digital.

Jolly, R. (2016). Happy at the top. *Harvard Business Review*, October 2016.

Loehr, J. and Schwartz, T. (2001). The making of a corporate athlete. *Harvard Business Review*, January 2001.

Ovans, A. (2015). What resilience means, and why it matters. *Harvard Business Review*, 5 January 2015.

Pemberton, C. (2015). *Resilience: A Practical Guide for Coaches*. New York, NY: McGraw Hill Education.

* **Schwartz, T. and McCarthy, C. (2007). Manage your energy, not your time. *Harvard Business Review*, October 2007.**

Chapter 11: Inspiration over a lifetime

Fels, A. (2004). Do women lack ambition? *Harvard Business Review*, April 2004.

* **Gratton, L. and Scott, A. (2016).** *The 100-Year Life*. **London: Bloomsbury**.

Buford, B. (2008). *Half Time: Moving from Success to Significance*. Grand Rapids, MI: Zondervan.

Johnson, L. (2016). If you want to leave a legacy, try the demon drink. *The Sunday Times*, 19 June 2016

Percy, S. (2016). *Who holds the key to closing the skills gap*? Ernst & Young.

Rohr, R. (2011). *Falling Upward: A Spirituality for the Two Halves of Life*. Kindle edition: Jossey-Bass.

* **Seligman, M. E. P. (2011).** *Flourish: A New Understanding of Happiness and Wellbeing*. **Kindle edition: Nicholas Brealey**.

Chapter 12: Inspiring others

Bains, G. (2011). *Meaning Inc: The Blueprint for Business Success in the 21st century*. Kindle edition: Profile.

Brann, A. (2015). *Engaged: The Neuroscience Behind Creating Productive People in Successful Organisations*. Kindle edition: Palgrave Macmillan.

Csikszentmihalyi, M. (2003). *Good Business: Leadership, Flow and the Making of Meaning*. New York: Penguin.

Felfe, J. and Schyns, B. (2014). Romance of leadership and motivation to lead. *Journal of Managerial Psychology*, 29(7), pp. 850–65.

Gino, F. (2016). Let your workers rebel. *Harvard Business Review*, October 2016.

* **Goffee, R. and Jones, J. (2006).** *Why should anyone be led by you?* **Boston, MA: Harvard Business Review Press**.

Goffee, R. and Jones, J. (2016). *Why should anyone work here?* Kindle edition: Harvard Business Review Press.

* **McKee, A., Boyatzis, R. and Johnston, F. (2008).** *Becoming a Resonant Leader*, **Kindle edition, Boston, MA: Harvard Business School**.

Nobel, C. (2015). Men want powerful jobs more than women do. *Harvard Business School, Working Knowledge*, 23 September 2015.

Owen, H. (2000). *The Power of Spirit: How Organisations Transform*. San Francisco, CA: Berret-Koehler.

Radlinska, A. and Pessiki, S. (2014). *The Human Era @ Work*, www. theenergyproject.com.

Scouller, J. (2011). *The Three Levels of Leadership*. Cirencester, UK: Management Books.

INDEX